SpringerBriefs in Po

More information about this series at http://www.springer.com/series/10047

D. Nicole Farris

Boomerang Kids:
The Demography of
Previously Launched Adults

 Springer

D. Nicole Farris
University of West Alabama
Livingston, AL, USA

ISSN 2211-3215   ISSN 2211-3223   (electronic)
SpringerBriefs in Population Studies
ISBN 978-3-319-31225-5   ISBN 978-3-319-31227-9   (eBook)
DOI 10.1007/978-3-319-31227-9

Library of Congress Control Number: 2016938692

© Springer International Publishing Switzerland 2016
This work is subject to copyright. All rights are reserved by the Publisher, whether the whole or part of the material is concerned, specifically the rights of translation, reprinting, reuse of illustrations, recitation, broadcasting, reproduction on microfilms or in any other physical way, and transmission or information storage and retrieval, electronic adaptation, computer software, or by similar or dissimilar methodology now known or hereafter developed.
The use of general descriptive names, registered names, trademarks, service marks, etc. in this publication does not imply, even in the absence of a specific statement, that such names are exempt from the relevant protective laws and regulations and therefore free for general use.
The publisher, the authors and the editors are safe to assume that the advice and information in this book are believed to be true and accurate at the date of publication. Neither the publisher nor the authors or the editors give a warranty, express or implied, with respect to the material contained herein or for any errors or omissions that may have been made.

This Springer imprint is published by Springer Nature
The registered company is Springer International Publishing AG Switzerland

Contents

Chapter 1
Introduction to Boomerang Children: Prevalence and Potential Questions

Abstract Young adults are moving back into their family homes and are now living with their parents. Common terms for the adult children include "previously launched adult" and "incompletely launched adult." According to data from the 2000 U.S. Census, in 1970 12.5 million 18–34 year olds lived at home, whereas in 2000 17.8 million 18–34 year olds lived at home (Furman, Boomerang nation: How to survive living with your parents… The second time around. Fireside, New York, 2005). A recent profile of the U.S. based on 2000 census data described our country as having about 67 million young adults aged 18–34. If 17.8 million of these young adults are living back at home, this is not an insignificant percentage. This chapter introduces the reader to the social phenomenon of the previously launched adult and provides an in depth description of these young adults. This chapter also details why these young adults are sociologically significant while providing information about young and emerging adulthood.

Keywords Family • Children • Parents • Adults • Demography • Statistics • Qualitative

College graduates and other young adults are moving with increased frequency back into their family homes and are living with their parents. According to data from the 2000 U.S. Census, in 1970 12.5 million 18–34 year olds lived at home, whereas in 2000 17.8 million 18–34 year olds lived at home (Furman 2005). A profile of the U.S. based on 2000 census data described our country as having about 67 million young adults aged 18–34. If 17.8 million of these young adults are living back at home, this is not an insignificant percentage. Indeed, as of 2013, 30 %, or just under one- third of all young adults are living at home with their parents (US Bureau of the Census 2014). Attributable factors include financial problems such as credit card and student loan debt, dismal job opportunities and a tight job market, economic downturn, low salaries for entry-level jobs and high housing costs (Furman 2005). Some more traditional demographic factors include factors such as a delay in the average age of marriage for both men and women, multiculturalism, and the emphasis on intergenerational living. With multiculturalism, some traditional ethnic groups are still morally opposed to cohabitation and delayed home leaving has become increasingly common and is more likely among traditional ethnic groups due to cultural traditions (Landale and Oropesa 2007; Mitchell 2009). In

© Springer International Publishing Switzerland 2016

D.N. Farris, *Boomerang Kids: The Demography of Previously Launched Adults*,
SpringerBriefs in Population Studies, DOI 10.1007/978-3-319-31227-9_1

addition to the more traditional leanings of particular ethnic groups, other groups may find that changing economic opportunities make living at home a preferred lifestyle.

In the past, during periods in the family life cycle known as the "launching" and "empty nest" periods, social norms dictated that adult children in the United States were expected to move out on their own, get married, and start a family (Clemens and Axelson 1985). Now, with such a large number of young adults still living at home, common terms have developed for these adult children such as "previously launched adult" and "incompletely launched adult" (Schnaiberg and Goldenberg 1989). A recent article in *The New York Times Magazine* discussed the issue of the "failure to launch" and "boomerang kids" (Henig 2010: 30). Television shows and other media sources are featuring grown children moving back in with their parents. For example, a cover of "The New Yorker" from last spring prominently depicted this trend. A young man hangs up his new Ph.D. in his childhood bedroom and has a cardboard box at his feet. This appears to be happening in many different kinds of families. Not only is the trend of adult children moving back home becoming more common, but young people also seem to be taking longer to reach adulthood. Whereas during the middle of the twentieth century young adulthood consisted of the transitions of completing school, leaving home, becoming financially independent, marrying, and having a child, these days many young adults are completing these transitions later in life or not completing them at all. Jeffrey Arnett, a psychologist from Clark University has suggested that society "views the 20s as a distinct life stage, call[ed] "emerging adulthood" (2010: 30). This stage of "emerging adulthood" contains aspects such as identity exploration, instability, and self-focus.

In most industrialized countries, the time period from the late teens through the twenties are years of profound change and importance (Arnett 2000). In the early part of their twenties, young people are obtaining the education and work training that will provide the foundation for the rest of their adult lives. Also occurring during this time are fluctuations in residence, employment and relationships. Presently, young adults seem to be caught in a sort of limbo between childhood and adulthood. For example, at age 18 people can vote and join the military, but they cannot drink until age 21. People who are full time students are considered "dependents" by the Internal Revenue Service and can continue to stay on their parents' health insurance plans until age 26. It seems that society is unable to agree upon when it is that someone is old enough to take on full adult responsibilities. Although many believe that there is a definite timeline, it does not appear to simply be a matter of age. Some scholars (see Rosenfeld 2007) have argued that the notion of a "boomerang effect" is fictional. Rosenfeld believes that young adults are living on their own and that this trend has been increasing for young adults since the 1950s. While this may be true, the large percentage of adult children moving back in with their parents is a clear indication that the phenomenon of previously launched adults is something that deserves further attention, as there are statistics to show that adult children, are in fact, moving back in with their parents. Certainly, 26 % of a particular subpopulation is not something that is merely fiction. It is a truth of the contemporary nature of the family, and both this reality and the changing nature of the family will be discussed and analyzed in more detail throughout this book.

While this issue is being debated among scholars, one point is certain; young people are taking longer to reach adulthood, as defined in terms of completing requisite life transitions and this delay can have serious implications in a variety of ways. Whereas at one point in time, boomerangers would have been forced to suffer in silence, unaware that there were others out there in similar situations, this is no longer the situation. There are increasing numbers of reports about these adult children surfacing in a variety of outlets in the popular media and academic journals. The number of adult children who are moving back in with their parents, i.e., the "boomerang generation," is growing (Mitchell 1998). There are a few studies of adult children returning to the homes of their parents and the extent to which this affects the happiness of the parents (Clemens and Axelson 1985; Aquilino and Supple 1991; Mitchell 1998) there has been little research on the effects that such moves have on the children themselves and the kinds of factors that lead an adult child to move back in to the parental home. This book will discuss various theories and explanations set forth about this behavior and will estimate statistical models to better understand which theories are most appropriate or salient in predicting who is more likely to live back at home with their parents.

The family has had many transitions during the past half-century. Family relationships and structure are important variables that affect many aspects of individuals' lives and in turn may affect society at large. Additional importance lies in the fact that moving back home with parents after once leaving is certainly a disruption in the life course, and studies suggest that nest leaving may not be a one-time only event (Goldscheider and DeVanzo 1985). The life course perspective and its implications related to this particular research are also of relevance.

1.1 More About Boomerang Children

Mitchell (2006) has argued that "dramatic changes are taking place in the lives of young adults, whom we conceptualize as members of the 'boomerang age'" (1). This description reflects the fact that compared to their predecessors today's young people often experience more movement in and out of a variety of family related roles, statuses, and living arrangements. As previously stated, there are a variety of contributing factors that may lead to the fluidity of the lives of the members of the "boomerang age." These include public factors such as the economy, the education system, and the job market, as well as more private considerations such as changing family forms and structures and varying and more egalitarian gender roles, which have resulted in women giving more priority to their education and careers, which leads them to postpone marriage and divorce (Mitchell 2006).

We see that as a result of the dynamic, complex, and fluid nature of family and intergenerational relationships and structures, the traditional notion of young adult transitions may become stalled and even reversed. To illustrate, we see the increase of the phenomenon of the "boomerang child," where young adults return to the parental home at least once after the initial departure. Returning to the parental home could have a variety of consequences for both the "boomerang child" and the family. Despite the fact that there have been numerous media and academic descriptions and depictions of these boomerang children, it could well be that these children feel to some extent disenfranchised, alone, and alienated from the rest of the world. Furman (2005) has argued that there are many misconceptions regarding boomerang children, such as the following: moving home means the adult child is a failure and that they are not mature adults; moving home will stunt emotional and psychological growth, and that it is stigmatic and shameful to need family support as an adult. In fact, it was these kinds of stereotypes that led me to conduct research on previously launched adults, and how moving back in with their parents would affect their identity, self-esteem, and self- concept.

Young adults who return home are often depicted as social and economic failures who are unable to fulfill parental expectations of autonomy (Mitchell 1998), which could have a deleterious effect on their identity, self-esteem, and self-concept. My prior research draws on identity theory and theories of self-esteem and self-appraisal to explore the consequences of moving back home with parents. Identity theory has a long standing history in the writings of George Herbert Mead and Charles Horton Cooley with their proposals that feedback from significant others provides the basis for individuals' self appraisals (Lundgren 2004). Self-appraisals can be understood as the "cognitive and evaluative components of self reference that are presumed to occur reflexively through a process of role taking" (2004: 269). Mead (1934) argued that we see ourselves as we think other see us, and Cooley (1902) observed that the reactions of others provide the viewpoint from which we come to define our attributes. We tend to use cues, clues, and feedback from others to construct and modify our behavior and beliefs in certain groups and situations (Hogg and Reid 2006).

The concept of identity includes not only the personal identity but also includes various group and social identities embedded in different networks (Howard 2000).

Self-esteem is an important component of one's identity. Self-esteem is an individual's overall positive evaluation of self. People seek to maintain or increase their self-esteem and tend to do so by putting themselves in situations that will promote self-verification (Cast and Burke 2002). Self-esteem can be understood as a central component of basic identity processes, and the desire for self-esteem motivates individuals to seek both verifying and enhancing social relationships (Cast and Burke 2002). Self-esteem is the function of two processes: the reflected appraisals of significant others in one's social environment in the form of social approval, and the individual's feelings of efficacy and competence derived from his or her own perceptions of the effects he or she has on his or her environment (Franks and Marolla 1976). An important issue pertinent to self- esteem is the fact that having good self esteem helps one persist in the face of failure, difficult situations, and can cause better performance, interpersonal success, happiness and even healthier lifestyles (Baumeister et al. 2003; Crocker et al. 2006).

My research suggests that most of the respondents did not in fact suffer from poor self-esteem as a result of moving back in with their parents, based on their responses to the questions I asked them related to how they felt about themselves and moving back home. Although I had no formal self-esteem measure, it seemed to be the case that the respondents did not experience negative effects from moving back home. However, each of them seemed to offer what Goffman (1963) referred to as stigma management techniques. Stigma refers to something unusual and bad about the moral status of the signifier. The term, according to Goffman, refers to an attribute that is deeply discrediting. Respondents also seemed to offer rationalizations for the behavior. Matza and Sykes (1957) have described techniques of neutralization that individuals use to justify actions in terms of rationalizations. Rationalizations are developed subsequent to deviant behavior (in this case, moving back home with one's parents), and rationalizations are offered to "protect the individual from self-blame and the blame of others after the act" (1957: 666).

1.2 Young and Emerging Adulthood

An event such as moving back home with parents can be more or less stigmatizing based upon the context in which it occurs. Sweeping demographic shifts have taken place over the past 50 years that have made young adulthood a distinctive period in the life course, rather than merely a period of brief transition from childhood to adulthood (Arnett 2000). The median age at first marriage has increased from the very early twenties (21 for women and 23 for men) in 1970 to a median age at first marriage of 26 for women and 28 for men in 2010 (U.S. Bureau of the Census Table of Median Age at First Marriage 2010b). When my grandmother was born in 1920, her mother and father were 18 and 22, respectively, so they were certainly even younger when they married. The trend of delayed age at first marriage is now mirrored by the age at first childbirth; moreover, the numbers of young Americans obtaining higher education after high school have risen as well (Arnett 2000). Additionally, life expectancy in the developed world has been on the rise and is mostly due to the increased prevention and control of the chronic diseases that affect adults, particularly heart disease and stroke. As of 2006, the life expectancy in the United States was about 78 years. In some other developed countries, life expectancy is as high as 81 or 82 (Poston and Bouvier 2010). Life spans are stretching longer and longer, and it may be prudent for young people in their 20s to experiment with their lives before making permanent decisions that will affect them for the next half-century.

These aforementioned changes have profoundly altered the development during the late teens and early twenties for many young people in industrialized societies. It is no longer normative for the late teens and early twenties to be a time of entering and settling into long-term adult roles. To the contrary, this period is associated with more frequent change and the personal exploration of various life directions. Demographers have become more conscious of the complexity of human behavior. Indeed, Rindfuss (1991) has noted precisely this trend in his review of the numerous topics examined at the annual Population Association of America meetings; topics such as care giving, household division of labor, child rearing, the empty nest, retirement, and a variety of others are now common topics for discussion whereas they were not part of the program a decade or more ago. At one point, Rindfuss argued, "these would have been inconceivable population topics for an earlier generation of demographers" (1991: 493). Rindfuss' words ring true because, traditionally, demographers concentrated solely on the more straightforwardly demographic events or transitions, such as births, deaths, migrations, and marriages. These demographic transitions are important, as they are the basic building blocks of population change. Contemporary demography, however, seeks to expand the range of social behavior under examination and includes a variety of topics such as the roles and activities related to the major demographic events. A closer examination of the period of young adulthood is important demographically because this period can have major effects on the traditional demographic processes.

According to Rindfuss (1991), the sequence of roles or activities experienced by young adults can be similar or diverse, and the sequences may or may not occur in a socially mandated order. The transitions during this period can be clear-cut or ambiguous and the young adult years represent a series of multiple transitions that are "demographically dense" (Rindfuss 1991: 494). By this, he means that more demographic action occurs during these years than during any other stage in the life course. For example, two of the three major demographic events reach their peak during the young adult years (fertility and migration). Fertility rates are almost uniformly high during the twenties, as are residential mobility rates. Also, during the young adult years, divorces occur much more frequently that at older ages. During the young adult years, persons acquire more education, fill new occupations, and their actions provide multiphasic demographic responses (Davis 1963).

Also ambiguous is the time period used to refer to the "young adult years." As I have done, Rindfuss also has marked the lower age boundary at age 18, as this is an age often recognized by the law for various activities and issues. Where Rindfuss and I diverge, however, is with respect to the upper cutoff of young adulthood. I argue that 34 is an appropriate age for cutoff, mainly because previous studies and the U.S. Census Bureau use the upper limit of 34 to cap the end year of young adulthood. Rindfuss' upper extreme is 30 years old because, he has stated, "30 represents the end of the young adult years… and the 30th birthday is often a time for taking stock and is used in questions addressed to young people about their adult occupational expectations" (1991: 494). Although Rindfuss' assessment of the upper boundary of the young adult years makes sense and is appealing from a chronological approach, I feel that my bounding the adult years at 34 is equally advantageous.

The diversity and variability in the young adult years can have a variety of consequences, both for those living in these years and those persons who are related to the young adults. Because so many people have a stake in the paths followed by young adults in the work, school and family spheres, and there are certain prescriptions regarding the sequence of these paths and the desirability of certain activities over others; these show the importance for further study of young adults and the transitions in their lives. This book seeks to examine the particular transition of home leaving during the young adult years, and the factors that lead to young adults either never leaving the family home, leaving the family home but then returning, or leaving the family home and not returning.

In the next chapter of the book, I review the relevant literature on this topic. I point to specific voids in the literature that I will endeavor to address in this work.

Chapter 2
Boomerang Children in the U.S.: History, Geography, and Household Characteristics

Abstract In this chapter I review the relevant literature pertaining generally to the coresidence of young adults in their parental households; I then discuss in some detail the theoretical foundations for my analyses. Before presenting my review of the general literature I first discuss some general issues pertaining to the coresidence of adult children. This chapter details the prior literature on the topic of previously launched adults, which, as stated, has frequently only described adult-parent coresidence situations where the child is possibly caring for an aging parent. The literature also predominantly focused on the parents rather than the children in these living arrangements. This chapter outlines the historical background of marriage and family structure in America and introduces readers to the theoretical foundations used in this book—namely, the life course perspective and perspectives relating to family development and household structure.

Keywords Family • Children • Parents • Life course • Household • Coresidence

In this chapter I review the relevant literature pertaining generally to the coresidence of young adults in their parental households; I then discuss in some detail the theoretical foundations for my analyses. Before presenting my review of the general literature I first discuss some general issues pertaining to the coresidence of adult children.

2.1 General Considerations About the Coresidence of Adult Children

Many studies about the coresidence of adult children, especially those dealing with the levels of parental happiness, do not differentiate between children who have returned home and children who never left (Mitchell 1998). Research shows that having an adult child return home can have a wide range of impacts on family well-being as a whole. Numerous television sources and books have portrayed adult children returning home in a somewhat negative light (Mitchell 1998). The media

© Springer International Publishing Switzerland 2016
D.N. Farris, *Boomerang Kids: The Demography of Previously Launched Adults*,
SpringerBriefs in Population Studies, DOI 10.1007/978-3-319-31227-9_2

tends to depict these adult children as being a generation that is "uniquely slow in establishing independence from parents" (White 1994: 82). This may be due in part to the fact that there is a widespread idea that leaving the parental home is one of the first major transitions in adulthood, and if this transition is delayed or disrupted, there may be some negative consequences for both the parents and the child (Billari and Liefbroer 2007).

In light of the recent economic recession, as well as factors such as high unemployment rates and costs of living, living away from home may be more difficult for adult children these days. Additionally, parents may not only have greater acceptance toward their children moving back home, but may also anticipate "patterns of prolonged dependence" from their adult children (Mitchell and Gee 1996: 443). The return of an adult child to the family home may also have negative implications for parents' marital satisfaction, or their satisfaction in general. Parents with poor health, blended families, lower socioeconomic status and higher numbers of children already living in the parental home could well have lower levels of satisfaction (Mitchell and Gee 1996).

Coresidence is almost always more beneficial for the child than for the parent and research shows some contradictions in the general findings regarding parents' feelings on living with their adult child. For example, Mitchell and Gee (1996) found that parents had negative reactions to their adult children returning home when the children left and returned multiple times and when children left the home the first time for work or school. The return of an adult child often created a financial and psychological burden for the parents. The once "empty nest" was now a "crowded nest," and some parents felt that the return of their child represented failure of themselves as parents (Schnaiberg and Goldenberg 1989; Aquilino 1990). The parents who reported unhappiness frequently noted that there was interpersonal conflict or turmoil between themselves and the child. Parents noted that a major factor affecting their happiness was the child's main activity at the time of coresidence; children who were working or attending school were thought to be less stressful to parents than those who were unemployed (Mitchell and Gee 1996). Parents also reported having problems with lack of privacy and independence, and the child's messiness or unwillingness to help with chores or other household tasks. Parents suggested that they sometimes felt their child was taking advantage of them in terms of financial support, which confirmed prior research that argued that adult children reaped more benefits from living at home than did parents when children were living back at home (Mitchell 1998). Previous studies also suggested that sons increased household demands while daughters may have been more likely to help around the house, and that sons provided less enjoyable interaction and companionship than daughters (Mitchell 1998).

Despite the findings, these data also described a high percentage of parents who were generally happy and experienced satisfaction despite the fact that their adult children were returning home. Parents received satisfaction as a result of the direct parent–child relationships (Aquilino and Supple 1991). In these cases, if the child helped with housework and other tasks and if the child and parents enjoyed positive interpersonal interactions, then the likelihood of parental happiness was much greater (Mitchell 1998). Mitchell also noted that parents reported a better assessment of living arrangements if the child and the parent engaged in fewer hostile arguments, if the child provided instrumental support, and if there were fewer disagreements with the "boomerang child" about getting along with other family members. Parents who experienced satisfaction with an adult child returning home also noted the enjoyment of companionship or friendship and having the family together. Even if there were some negative effects of an adult child returning home, these could frequently be lessened if the child had taken on some aspect of a traditional adult role, such as engaging in full time employment. A poignant quote from one study regarding adult children living at home stated that "it is not whether an adult child lives at home, but which adult child lives at home" that will be the most salient in determining parental happiness with adult child coresidence (White 1994:94).

Additionally, research using data from the Survey of Income and Program Participation (SIPP) to analyze parent and child coresidence, focused on the perspective and experience of the parent rather than the child. Speare and Avery (1992) analyzed instances of elderly persons living with older children and looked specifically at parents' transitions to and from coresidence with their children, rather than the transition of the children to and from coresidence with their parents. They found that driving forces that compelled parents to live with their adult children tended to focus on the needs of elderly people based on their health and disability status. If for example, an elderly person needed help with daily activities, he or she would be more likely to move in with and remain living with adult children.

Likewise, Aquilino (1990) analyzed and estimated the likelihood of parent and adult child coresidence by concentrating on characteristics relating to family structure and other parental characteristics. Aquilino found that parental dependency was not the major factor that explained coresidency at any point in the life course, and this finding is similar to the findings from previous research. Parental and family structure characteristics did have effects on whether or not an adult child would move home; parents' marital dissolution and subsequent remarriage were negatively related to adult child coresidence, while parents with extended households (including the presence of relatives or nonrelatives in the household) significantly increased the likelihood of having adult children as coresidents (Aquilino 1990). While the literature focusing on the experiences of the parents is interesting and informative, it leaves a large gap in the body of knowledge regarding previously launched adults. Additionally, a majority of these studies are somewhat outdated, published in the 1980s and early 1990s, and while these studies can inform future research, I believe that more research is needed to fully assess the phenomenon of previously launched adults. I turn next to the general literature on marriage and family structure.

2.2 Historical Background of Marriage and Family Structure in America

While the phenomenon of adult children living at home is not new to the American family, the fact that adult children are doing so during a time in which we are so highly independent and individualistic as a society is something that warrants further consideration. Census data have showed that intergenerational coresidence was maintained throughout the industrial revolution, and during this period of time, young adults almost always lived with their parents or with parental surrogates. Intergenerational coresidence began to decline after World War II and many other aspects of family life changed a great deal during the industrial revolution. For example, infant mortality declined, fertility declined, household size declined, the divorce rate increased, and millions of people moved away from farming and began to work in the factories (Rosenfeld 2007). These changes, as well as others, are largely still in effect to the present day. Other changes that occurred after World War II and have had a lasting impact on Americans include the rise of divorce and heterosexual cohabitation, the invention of the birth control pill, the sexual revolution, the civil rights movement, the rise of feminism and women's rights, and the gay rights movement. Rosenfeld (2007) noted that the ordinary and traditional life course transition used to consist of first living with one's parents and then living with one's spouse. Historically, one was almost always part of a family, either headed by the parents or in a marital family with children. In fact, singlehood was so abnormal, that bachelors could not legally live on their own without special permission in several American colonies. This was due in large part to the fear of the absence of social control that is to some degree always present in the family. Rosenfeld argued that in order to understand the dynamics of intergenerational relationships, it was important to understand how family structures of the past impacted the mate selection of young adults, historically speaking.

Cherlin (2009) has described the history of marriage and how marriage in the United States was so much vastly different than marriage in any of the other Westernized nations. In the United States, we have largely taken for granted that love and marriage go hand in hand. Cherlin, however, noted that this has actually not always been the case. Prior to the twentieth century, love was not a precondition for marriage and was actually considered to be risky business for marriage. In the nineteenth century, people engaged in more utilitarian type marriages, and in order to protect their livelihood they strove to marry someone who would be able to work on the family farm or take care of the family. If someone married for love, and the person turned out to not be a good provider, then the family could be left in the wake of a serious destruction.

The idea of utilitarian marriage seemed to lose its appeal in the late 1800s and early 1900s. During this time was a shift toward a more companionate type of marriage, one that was based more on intimacy and the loving feelings of two people for one another. As we know, marrying for love and love only is not an event that really happens; parents and communities have always influenced the mate choices of young adults and these choices are constrained by various structural factors. Factors such as social, legal, and demographic forces often create a narrow pool of people from which to choose a potential mate. Social and demographic constraints exist via residential segregation, intergenerational coresidence, closed labor markets, and early age at first marriage (Rosenfeld 2007). Residential segregation ensures homogamy, or marrying or mating with individuals with similar characteristics, and this is due to the fact that residential segregation almost always is based on racial characteristics. Racial residential segregation greatly reduces interracial social exposure, thus leading to a lower likelihood of meeting and marrying. Clearly, young adults who live at home face increased inputs from their parents about their potential mates; this could potentially lead to more traditional unions.

In the mid 1900s we saw a specific type of family form arise, that of the husband headed and male breadwinner ideal. Though many people recall this time fondly, such a familial configuration was not actually the norm for American family life. During the 1800s women greatly helped out and worked to support the family, whether it was by working on the family farm or doing other tasks to help contribute to the family livelihood. During the 1950s there was some tension between the idea of companionate marriage and the male breadwinner ideal; however divorce rates were extremely low and marriage rates were quite high. The male breadwinner ideal somewhat lost favor after the 1950s, particularly during the 1960s and 1970s with all the social and cultural changes that were occurring in the United States. These included events such as the Civil Rights Movement and the sex and gender revolutions. Additionally, this was a time when women were entering the paid labor force en masse, and their increased labor force participation also greatly changed the way we viewed marriage and family situations.

The 1980s brought the rise of individualized and expressive marriage, that is, marriage in which people thought and felt that they should be personally fulfilled in every aspect of life, including the marriage. If a marriage was somehow unfulfilling, the partners should have the right to end it. This led to the 1990s where we saw a steady high rate of divorce, and we really have not turned around from this even over 20 years later. These ideas of marriage that emerged in the latter half of the twentieth century are what in effect lead to what Cherlin has termed "the Marriage Go Round." It seems to be the case that Americans hold two very different ideals when it comes to marriage. These ideals are that most Americans, when asked, say that they believe a marriage should last forever, and also that their marriage would last forever. However and quite contrarily, the same people who expressed these assertions about marriage lasting forever also claim that they agreed with the idea that those who were unhappy in a marriage should get a divorce. America seems to be the only country that has these two conflicting ideals occurring at once in the same person. In other countries, there may be the idea that marriage is quite important and that marriage will last forever, but it is not in tandem with the idea that an unhappy person should get divorced. Likewise, in those countries that agree with the assertion that unhappy people should get divorced, they are not in agreement that marriage is so important and that everyone should aspire to get married and be married forever.

Changing notions of marriage seem to go hand and hand with alternative and changing families and family structures as well as changes in individual ideals. Rosenfeld has argued that "from the individual perspective, the family always seems to be changing" (2007: 42). As far as family structures are concerned, we have seen an increase in every type of nontraditional union. The numbers of interracial, same sex and heterosexual cohabiting couples have been growing since 1960 (Rosenfeld 2007). The reality of the contemporary family is that the "traditional" nuclear family is but one of many variations of family structure and household structure. In addition to single parent families, interracial, same sex, and heterosexual cohabiting couples, more people are choosing to remain single. Historically, failure to marry was linked to perceptions about personal or social deficiencies. Similar to the stigmas relating to "boomerang children," these stigmas about singlehood are fast disappearing. Many young people no longer view marriage as necessarily better than remaining single and the number of single people reporting that they are "very happy" has increased steadily in the last three decades. As the current generation of never married people age, it is likely that many will remain unmarried and forego childbearing. Those who do forego childbearing are likely to still be faced with a pro-child social message. Those who choose not to do so, especially women, continue to be denigrated or regarded as selfish or incomplete. While some single parents naturally include divorced parents, there is also an escalating subset of highly educated women who choose motherhood but not marriage.

It is important to note that the role of critical historical eras and events are very important for our being able to understand the trends associated with home leaving and returning. Historical events, such as the Industrial Revolution, World War II and the Great Depression, as well as longer term changes in the attractiveness of living with parents, family structure, the growth of second rate jobs, and other factors, have lead to a high increase in the likelihood of returning home (Goldscheider and Goldscheider 1999). Between 1880 and 1940, the percentage of single young adults who lived with their parents increased (Rosenfeld 2007). This was likely due in part to the increasing life expectancy of older Americans. As life expectancy increased, more and more unmarried young adults lived with their parents simply because there were more parents available with whom to live. Additionally, living with parents was normative, and there were few other practical options. Conversely, researchers have argued that during the Depression there were likely unstable finances and home situations that may have resulted in a lower likelihood of adult children moving home with their parents.

In the mid-twentieth century, the long-established norm of intergenerational co-residence began to change, even as parents were living longer and longer. Despite the fact that more adult children had living parents, the percentage of adult children living with their parents began to decline. World War II had a profound impact on young men's transitions to adulthood, and young men who reached the age of 18 between 1938 and 1944 left home for the first time to join the military service, compared with barely one in six who joined the military among those who reached the age of 18 between 1930 and 1937 (the Depression era) (Goldscheider and Goldscheider 1999). Non-family related leaving was temporarily interrupted by the marriage component of the baby boom, but thereafter other non-family routes out of the home began to increase. Non- family reasons for leaving included attending college away from home, and leaving home solely to be independent. Those persons who came of age between 1968 and 1972 had the highest surges or non-family leaving, as well as those who came of age later in the 1970s. This trend faded somewhat in the 1980s, likely due to increases in housing costs, and this is important because it seems as though the trend of home leaving and returning has continued throughout the years until the present.

Since 1960, the independent life stage has become increasingly routine for young adults in the United States (Rosenfeld 2007). The independent life stage overturned old norms (namely, the norm of adult children living with parents), and now both parents and children expect to achieve some measure of independence. Contemporarily, a major contributor to the increase in rates of returning home may be the changes related to the nest leaving process itself (Goldscheider and Goldscheider 1999). Research has shown that returning home was more likely among those who left at a young age or those who left home for reasons other than marriage. Reasons other than marriage include leaving home simply to be independent, getting a degree, or taking a job. The decline in age at leaving home is important to examine as well because young adults usually leave the family home during late adolescence or young adulthood. As a result, they have likely not had experience in adult economic or social roles and thus may be more likely to return to the family home.

Mitchell (2009) has noted that two trends of particular importance have surfaced to create the "boomerang age." These are the greater instability and reversibility of partnership formation, and the increased likelihood that once young adults leave the family home, they are not precluded from returning. There are indeed changing notions of marriage and family and many young people are likely to question or even rebel against traditional behavior. Nevertheless, the U.S. has become increasingly multicultural and some families may even display patterns of behavior consistent with their cultural traditions. For example, some traditional ethnic groups are still morally opposed to cohabitation and delayed home leaving has become increasingly common and is more likely among traditional ethnic groups due to cultural traditions (Landale and Oropesa 2007; Mitchell 2009). In addition to the more traditional leanings of particular ethnic groups, other groups may find that changing economic opportunities make living at home a preferred lifestyle.

Billari and Liefbroer (2007) have poignantly discussed the potential influences and impacts of age norms on leaving home. As leaving the parental home is arguably one of the most important and first major transitions during young adulthood, social norms dictate that the time of leaving home should be influenced by how individuals, particularly young adults, feel about these norms. There are a variety of determinants that impact the age at which young adults leave the family home; Billari and Liefbroer discussed three of them. The first determinant is related to the involvement in parallel events that would coincide with a young adult moving out of the home; these include getting a job, going to college, or getting married. Often involvement with one of the aforementioned events results in a decision to leave home. The second determinant deals with the opportunities and constraints that might have led to or impeded the decision to leave the parental home. These opportunities and constraints have been previously mentioned, and include housing market and economic conditions. The third determinant is related to the impact of cultural factors, attitudes, and values. The importance of social norms for decision-making during young adulthood has been stressed within the life course approach, which will be discussed in much more detail later in this book.

Some researchers have argued that age norms can only be considered norms if they are backed up by sanctions. However, it was unlikely that sanctions were attached to age norm transgressions, and even if there were sanctions attached it would be hard to tell what these sanctions were. Sanctions were unlikely followed through with regard to age norms because it appeared that age norms were generally followed regardless of whether or not there were sanctions associated with age norm transgressions. Additionally, the exact timing of age norms seemed to be unclear; should the age norm occur at a precise age or within a range of certain ages? Studies (Veevers et al. 1996; Settersten 1998) have shown that a vast majority of young adults perceived an age deadline for certain transitions, namely leaving home. Age deadlines for leaving home were substantially shared by respondents, who themselves also agreed that there were no specific consequences attached to violations of these age norms.

Sociological and demographic literature on age norms suggests that "age norms may influence the occurrence and timing of important life course decisions but are not very helpful in explaining how norms relate to other factors that may influence home leaving" (Billari and Liefbroer 2007: 183). To account for the fact that age norms might not be helpful in explaining impacts of life course decisions, Billari and Liefbroer (2007) sought to maximize their explanation by incorporating Fishbein and Ajzen's (1975) theory of reasoned behavior. Essentially, the theory of reasoned behavior states that various factors tend to influence people's intentions and their behavior. These factors include attitudes or beliefs, subjective norms, and perceived behavioral control. These factors are determined by beliefs about whether or not others approved or disapproved of a particular behavior, in this case, the age at which someone left the family home. However, the social networks to which individuals belong also have an impact on societal norms. Billari and Liefbroer (2007) showed that perceived opinions of parents were associated with the actual timing of leaving the parental home and societal norms and friends' norms concerning the timing of leaving home were not. I turn next in this chapter to the theoretical foundations of my research.

2.3 Theoretical Foundations

A major conceptual approach I used to inform the research I undertook is the life course perspective. The life course perspective analyzes the relationship between norms, expectations, and the timing and sequencing of various events in and the life stages among individuals (Mitchell 1998). It directs our attention to the powerful connection between individual lives and the historical and socioeconomic contexts in which these lives unfold (Mitchell 2006). The basic idea is that social norms exist about the appropriate timing of major events in life (Billari and Liefbroer 2007). The life course is the course of aging, but also involves many facets and implications (Clausen 1972). Common events include going to school, getting a job, starting a family, and perhaps most importantly, gaining economic independence from parents. Theoretically, age is the determining factor that specifies appropriate times for the stages and transitions. Returning home when one is supposed to be moving onto a new transition throws traditional age transitions off schedule (Settersten and Hagestad 1996; Smith 2004).

It is important to note that different variations in social contexts, including family structure, background, and different demographic variables (such as race, gender, religion, occupation, and social class) can have profound ramifications on an individual's particular pattern in the life course. People compare themselves with their peers to draw conclusions about whether or not they are "on time" with respect to important life transitions (Billari and Liefbroer 2007). However, Elder (1985) has argued that the contexts in which adults are returning to the home of their parents (economic climates, delayed transitions of marriage and family) are helping to redefine the life transition and make returning home more normative.

A major question posed by life course theory that is relevant for this research is "how do collective experiences of birth cohort members generate structural change?" (Hess 1988: 16). In particular, if the collective experience of a particular cohort of young adults is that of moving back in with parents, this could perhaps produce a structural change in the family and how we view this institution. Elder and his colleagues have put forth an elaborated life course framework related to the individual and to family development (1998). This perspective argues that families were changed by the behavior and developmental courses of the members; subsequently it was important to pay attention to the transitions of the individuals that comprised a particular family. Additionally, important also was the notion that changing lives altered developmental trajectories (Elder 1998).

As previously mentioned, these trajectories or pathways include education, work, and family, and are followed by individuals and groups in society. Elder has argued that various historical forces "shape the social trajectories of family, education, and work, and they in turn influence behavior and particular lines of development" (1998: 2). Likewise, Mitchell (2006) has argued that an individual's own life path is embedded in and transformed by conditions and events occurring during the historical period and geographical location in which the person lives. Geopolitical events, economic cycles, and social and cultural ideologies can often shape people's perceptions and choices and alter the course of human development. I believe that the historical forces at work that need to be entertained in my research are the economic crises that have shaped the last ten or so years, most especially in the years between 2005 and 2010. Various contributing factors include the bursting of the housing bubble, sub-prime and predatory lending, and increased debt; indeed all may be active parts of history that would be historical factors that changed history in a negative way. We can see that all of these various interrelated parts are combined in a way that led to economic downturn; this in turn has led to decreased job opportunities for young adults, high student loan debt, and lack of viable prospects for the future.

An interesting part of the life course perspective emphasizes how human lives are interdependent and connected on various levels. Elder (1998) has described a situation of "linked lives" whereby societal and individual experience are linked through the family and its network of shared relationships. Consequently, macro-level events affect individual behaviors and this micro/macro link significantly affects familial relationships in a variety of ways. Mitchell (2006) has also noted that the idea of linked lives may be seen in the way that generational relations were interconnected with experiences and transitions from earlier life. Stages and transitions in the life course were interlocked across generations and existed within the context of different relationships and historical events.

While it may be argued that regardless of historical forces and economic atmospheres, individuals have agency to shape and control their own lives, ultimately the structures that are in place have a great impact on the choices and opportunities actually available to individuals in a given place and time. People and families are subject to the constraints imposed upon them as they live in particular sociohistorical locations. Being subject to various historical times and the consequences of these times could well lead to shared experiences of moving back home that could potentially have lasting impacts on the lives of these various young adults. Early life course decisions, opportunities, and conditions can affect later life outcomes for individuals (Mitchell 2006). The past has the ability to shape the present and the future, much like a domino effect, and this can occur on a cohort/generational level and also on an individual level. The timing and circumstances under which various early life events occur can potentially set up a "chain reaction" of experiences for individuals and their families and events experienced earlier in life may continue to influence an individual's life path in the future throughout the life course (Mitchell 2006).

Unfortunately owing to a lack of longitudinal data, it will not be possible for me in this project to determine such lasting effects. I need data from a longitudinal study that could follow cohorts throughout their lives to see exactly what X variables are related to moving back home. However, I am unable to perform such a study at this point in time. Despite this drawback, I will be able to examine other theoretically relevant variables relating to the life course, such as how many times the child has left and subsequently returned to the home, and how these returns affect both their and their parents' happiness.

Despite a shared experience, there is room for differences within cohorts. For example, some members of a particular cohort may experience the life course and its trajectories in a "traditional" manner. This would include moving out of the family home, getting an education, getting a job, getting married, and having a family. However, not everyone in a cohort may have a shared experience and experience the events in the same temporal order. I believe that this is why it is important to study such a group, and try to see what factors may lead to or detract from a particular life course of events and the temporal order in which these events occur.

From a demographic standpoint, the life course perspective is extremely important. When traditional life course trajectories are followed, individuals will likely marry and reproduce in the "normal" fashion. We now know that some groups are delaying marriage and childbearing until later years, and this may also be the case if parts of the life course are interrupted. For example, moving back home with a parent is likely to inhibit a young adult from procreating. Depending on the length of time an individual spends living back at home; the events of marrying and childbearing may well be delayed even more than previously assumed. Lastly, I think Mitchell made a poignant observation that with the life course approach there is "recognition of innovation and human agency in the life course. New behaviors, when routinized, can be created or alter pre-existing trends" (2006: 25). There is some speculation that behaviors such as home returning and cohabitation with parents have become and will continue to become increasingly popular, most likely due in part to the loss of social stigma that once existed when these types of behaviors were not widely practiced. It is my hope that this is the case, and that this phenomenon of adult children moving back in with their parents continues to lose social stigma, as it is in some cases an utmost necessity for young adults to move back in with their parents.

The family development framework is another theoretical perspective of relevance for my analysis. Aldous (1978) has argued that family development has focused on the characteristics of families over the period of their existence and also on the content and timing of past events in individual histories and how these events affect present interaction patterns among the family members. Historically, families expected a certain sequencing of family related events. For example, young people typically expected to complete schooling, marry before having children, and then later become grandparents. Patterns were so predictable that scholars found the depictions of family life and the life course of the family to be relatively accurate (Mitchell 2006). This is not always the case anymore. With recent changes, the timing and sequencing of events are too varied to warrant this linear model of family development. Indeed families may be involved in multiple stages simultaneously, may reverse stages, and might not fit into a model whatsoever.

Additionally, Aquilino has noted that "in the launching stage of the family life cycle, the developmental tasks of young adulthood involved relinquishing economic and emotional dependencies on parents" (1991: 14). Aldous (1978) has also contended that during this period parents have tended to shift their focus from parenting to reestablishing the marital relationship. However, as we well know, these requisite events during the launching cycle are often likely disrupted with the return of an adult child to the home. The ability to examine the feelings of parents regarding their adult children moving home, as well as the content and timing of individual events are of particular interest for this project, and with the available data I will be able to analyze this portion of the theory more closely.

Demographic theories of marriage and family are important to analyze the context of previously launched adults. Waite (2006: 87) has noted that "the family is one of the foundational social institutions in all societies, although the definition of the family varies from place to place and from time to time." Often, people use the term family when they really mean household, namely, all those sharing a dwelling. Household members may or may not be related by blood, marriage, or adoption. Conversely, "family" can refer to a number of different social entities and a variety of living arrangements. There are a variety of dimensions by which people view families. These include procreation, sexual relations, socialization, residence, economic cooperation, and emotional ties (Mitchell 2006).

Waite has also argued that the contemporary family in the United States looks different than it did in the past. Considerable diversity exists across and within families. Popular previous definitions of the family tended to emphasize that it was the basic institution of society, and that it was a social and economic unit consisting of "two adults of the opposite sex who shared economic resources, sexual intimacy, labor, accommodations, reproduction, and childrearing" (Mitchell 2006: 21). Fewer people today are living in traditionally defined families, with more living in non-family households. Most scholars recognize that previous definitions of the family were often idealized, ideologically based, and not always relevant to the realities of modern family life. This is attributable to transitions such as earlier nest leaving by young adults (as well as returning to the nest), delayed marriage, non-marriage, and marital disruption. Waite has noted that children have depended almost entirely on their families for financial, emotional, and instrumental support, but sometimes they failed to take intoaccount the age at which this support was supposed to end, and what ramifications could be seen if children continued to receive this support from their parents well into adulthood. Waite has also argued that with current debates about the characteristics of marriage and the family, it was necessary to continue with further research that could help contribute to understanding these changing notions and ideas.

Social capital is also important to consider when analyzing the life course. The ability to adapt to life course change can certainly vary according to the resources or support available to families or individuals. These resources can be either economic or cultural, and they are exceedingly important to consider when using a life course perspective. Originally developed by French theorist Pierre Bordieu in the 1970s, social capital is defined as "social connections among individuals" such that it "inheres in the structure of relations" (Bordieu 1986). Access to social capital can generate normative structures and resources, such as social support (Mitchell 2006). Social capital and social support can be seen in various groups that emphasize family centered norms, values, and obligations. Social capital can also be found within families and can stem from the quality of intergenerational relationships (Mitchell 2006). Young adults with weak family ties may not have the option to return home during difficult economic times, regardless of other types of capital (Mitchell 2000). This is an important and interesting way to look at capital with respect to previously launched adults, because it would likely be the case that when the issue of capital comes to mind, it is most likely economic capital. That being said, those who come from families with low economic capital may have different likelihoods of moving back in with parents, and this may also be dependent on the social capital of the family as well. Young adults approach their lives with a given set of personal characteristics that are intertwined with individual and family resources, and then combined with various other constraints. Moving back home with parents may seem like a purely individual decision, but it should actually be viewed through the lens of a much wider social context (Mitchell 2006).

As I have previously stated, young adults are social beings who have the potential to navigate and create their own lives and even in some cases instigate social change. However, the possibilities for those who lack social and economic capital (financial power, education, social networks) are much more limited. As a result, the life course and the events that occur within each individual's life course are neither entirely free creations nor entirely pre-determined, but a complex mix of the various components of macro and micro level circumstances that are occurring at a particular time and location.

There are a variety of factors that could contribute to or detract from the likelihood that a young adult would move back in with their parents. I intend to examine several factors related to various demographic, life course, and family related issues in order to better understand the relationships between these variables and the launching status of young adults.

2.4   Conclusion

It seems evident from the literature on previously launched adults that further analyses such as those to be undertaken in this book have merit and will contribute to the literature in a variety of areas. The extensive literature reported and reviewed on the topic of previously launched adults has served as a background for this research. To conclude, it seems that studies looking specifically at previously launched adults and the characteristics of these children themselves are sparse, and those that do exist typically date back many decades, with few contemporary counterparts. Therefore this book will also serve as an opportunity for reexamining the phenomenon and its relevance and applicability in more modern times. These analyses, hopefully, will also contribute to current literature in an important way: the launching status of adult children will differentiate between those who move out of the family home and then return and those who never move out of the family home.

This current chapter was a review of literature in several areas relevant to the research questions of this book. Before turning to the analyses intended to examine the research questions, I will discuss in the next chapter the data and methods that will be used in the analyses.

Chapter 3
Data and Methodology

Abstract This chapter describes the data and methodology used in this analysis. Data were gathered from the American Community Survey and the National Survey of Families and Households for the quantitative part of this study. Time is spent discussing the operationalization of the dependent variable and the rationale for utilizing multinomial logistic regression for this analysis. It describes the independent variables and the sample characteristics.

Keywords Statistics • Variable • Sample • ACS • NSFH • Data • Methodology

For the quantitative portion of this research, there were a number of different data sets that could have been used. The American Community Survey (ACS) employs annual estimates of the nation, regions, states, congressional districts, and many levels of geography. The collection period is every year and many of the data are released the year after the collection cycle. The ACS is conducted every year to provide up to date information about the social and economic needs of the community. The ACS is intended to show how people live; it examines education, jobs, housing, and other questions. The questionnaire items pertain to the relationship of all people to only the householder and are asked for all persons in households. The National Survey of Families and Households (NSFH) was designed to provide a broad range of information on family life to serve as a resource for research across disciplinary perspectives. It is a longitudinal survey of a national sample that is representative of American households. Life history information is collected in this survey, including the following: respondent's family living arrangements in childhood, departures and returns to the family home, and histories of marriage, cohabitation, education, fertility, and employment. The NSFH data are the ideal data to use for my research for a variety of reasons. Primarily, the survey contains questions regarding adult children leaving and returning to the family home and also includes other important topics related to my particular area of interest about parent–child relationships. I used the NSFH data for the bulk of my statistical analyses, but I also employed the ACS data to describe more recent trends of adult children living with their parents.

© Springer International Publishing Switzerland 2016

D.N. Farris, *Boomerang Kids: The Demography of Previously Launched Adults*, SpringerBriefs in Population Studies, DOI 10.1007/978-3-319-31227-9_3

3.1   History of the NSFH

According to Sweet and associates (1988: 1), researchers at the University of
Wisconsin responded to a request for proposals (RFP) distributed in June of 1983
by the Center for Population Research and the National Institute of Child Health
and Human Development. The RFP sought research proposals studying many
aspects of family life experience as both determinants and consequences of other
family and life course events. The research team (Larry Bumpass, James Sweet,
Maurice MacDonald, Sara McLanahan, Annemette Sorensen, and Elizabeth
Thomson) represented various disciplines and perspectives including family sociology, social demography, social psychology, and family economics. The researchers
were awarded the contract and then began developing the basic survey design and
question sequences. The researchers obtained a $4.8 million grant from the National
Institute of Health and Human Development to aid in the implementation of this
research project.

The project grew out of the experiences that various researchers had with the
limitations of available data on family structure, family processes and family relationships. Much of the data from other major national data sources had been collected for other purposes, and many of the available data sources were based on
samples that did not represent the total United States population. Many of the samples were samples of convenience and probability samples of one city or state.
Further, most of the other previous surveys focused on one specific family issue and
facilitated a detailed understanding of a particular topic, but did not enable researchers to study the context of the larger familial relationships. Additionally, these data
were often collected to speak to the concerns of one particular academic discipline
or were mainly based on one theoretical perspective.

3.2   The NSFH Sample

The NSFH main sample is a national, multi-stage area probability sample contain-
ing about 17,000 housing units drawn from 100 sampling areas in the conterminous
United States. A multistage probability sample is a complex random sample in
which units are first randomly sampled, and then the subunits of the sampled units
are randomly sampled, and so on (Treiman 2009). Examples include area probability samples in which cities and counties are randomly sampled, then blocks within
areas, then households within blocks, then persons within households. The goal of
the NSFH was to design a survey that (1) focused almost exclusively on family
issues, (2) covered a broad range of family structures, processes and relationships,
(3) was a national probability sample so that it would be possible to generalize to
the United States population, (4) was a sufficiently large enough sample to permit
subgroup comparisons and reliable statistical estimation, (5) spoke to issues important to a number of disciplines and sub-disciplines and to persons working from a

variety of theoretical perspectives, (6) would permit the testing of competing hypotheses concerning a variety of issues about the American family, and (7) addressed many of the most important cross sectional descriptive and analytic questions to provide respective reports of respondents' prior experience in both family and other life domains.

The researchers argued that a major goal of the NSFH was to document the nature and variability of American family life. The researchers felt there were a number of topics that were important and therefore should be covered in a comprehensive survey of family structure, process, and relationships. The researchers also felt there ought to be some measures from other previous national surveys that should be replicated. The researchers did this when the previously used questions appeared to give them adequate information, but they often opted to use the new survey as an opportunity for innovation in measurement. The NSFH interview and self-administered questionnaires were quite long. The main interview schedule included over 600 questions, many of which had several parts; the self-administered questionnaire was over 60 pages long. Many sections of the interview and self-administered questionnaire were asked only of a small portion of the total sample. The researchers attempted to design an interview with a mean length of 90 min or less. They performed pretests for a variety of reasons, including an attempt to obtain realistic timing estimates for various sections of the interview.

In the NSFH, individuals were the units of observation, rather than families or households. As previously discussed, the definition of household or family is quite complicated and varies over time. Using individuals as the unit of observation allowed for a clean and clear description of the family and household history of the reference individuals, their current circumstances, relationships and attitudes; this allowed the researchers to follow their subsequent experiences. They were able to describe the circumstances of households, families, marriages, and of adults and children in these units in the United States from the perspective of the reference individual. The researchers did not attempt to sample persons living in institutions or other group quarters due in part to logistical and cost considerations. However, in the sample, they did include as members of a household all persons who were "currently away at college" or "currently away in the Armed Forces" and "who live in a dorm, sorority, or fraternity house" or "in military housing or on a ship."

There were some substantively important subgroups for which the original sample size of 10,000 respondents was inadequate. Hence, the researchers oversampled some strategic population groups, including minorities, one-parent families, families with stepchildren, cohabiters, and recently married persons. These groups were oversampled for a variety of reasons. One-parent and reconstituted families were important because from both scientific and policy perspectives, understanding how one- parent families and stepfamilies function was and continues to be very important. There was little prior cross sectional research focusing on these compositions of families. The researchers thought it essential to be able to make contrasts among one-parent families, families with two natural parents, and families with stepchildren. Cohabiting couples represented at the time one of the more important family changes in recent decades, and a better understanding of cohabitation was essential for understanding contemporary marriage and family life; thus, cohabiters were included in the oversample. The researchers decided to oversample recently married persons in order to have a larger number of cases of groups exposed to the risk of important family transitions during the duration of the longitudinal study. Recently married persons have high rates of fertility, marital disruption, and other life cycle transitions. The oversample was accomplished by doubling the number of households selected within the 100 sampling areas.

3.2.1   Description of the NSFH

The NSFH included information related to household composition, goings and comings of children, relationships with adult children (asked of the head of household or the spouse), and also asked questions of the adult focal children. The questions posed to the parents dealt with a variety of issues, including household composition, household tasks, health, care giving and receiving, marriage and cohabitation, fertility history, problem inventory for children (including those aged 18–33), relationships with young adult focal children (of particular interest for this research), residential history, education, religion, employment and income. Variables of interest relating to the focal children included household composition, separations from biological parents, leaving/returning to parent's home, marital/cohabitation history, education, dating, fertility, relationship with mother/father/stepparent, employment, income, household tasks, happiness with marital/cohabiting relationship, social integration/support, religion, sexual activity, tobacco/alcohol use, and number and relationships with siblings. The NSFH was administered in three waves; from 1987 to 1988 (Wave 1), 1992 to 1994 (Wave 2), and 2001 to 2003 (Wave 3). I use data gathered in Wave 3 for this book.

3.2.2   Wave 3

As previously stated, the first wave of the NSFH was a national survey of 13,017 persons aged nineteen and over and included oversamples of minorities, single parent families, stepfamilies, recently married couples, and cohabiting couples (Sweet et al. 1988). In 1992–1994, the researchers re-interviewed 10,008 of the original respondents in face-to-face computer assisted interviews (Sweet and Bumpass 1995). Additionally, the researchers interviewed 6416 current or former spouses or partners and also conducted telephone interviews with 1416 children aged 10–17, 1090 sons and daughters aged 18–24, and 3348 parents. The response rate for the main sample was 82 % for eligible main respondents and about 80 % for spouses.

The University of Wisconsin Survey Center conducted the third wave of the NSFH. Due to budgetary restrictions, a subset of the NSFH Wave 1 sample was re-interviewed using CATI technology. At the time of Wave 3, 81 % of the sample was located, and of those located, 72% were interviewed. Over nine thousand (9230) main respondent, spouse, and focal child interviews were completed for the third wave of the NSFH. In addition, 924 proxy interviews were completed for main respondents who were deceased or too ill to complete the interview. The overall response rate was 57%. All interviews were conducted over the telephone using CATI technology. The CATI system used is known as CASES; in this system the text of the survey appears question by question on a computer screen for the interviewer to read to the respondent. Routing through the interview is based on skip logic pre-programmed into the computer. The system allows for pre-coded questions, open-ended questions and combinations of the two. In addition, the computer allows only valid responses; when an invalid response is entered, the computer asks the interviewer to reenter the response.

The instruments for the main respondents and their spouses were identical; focal children received a shorter interview. The content of the main respondent/spouse interview was essentially the same as the Wave 2 interview with some modifications. The focal child interview was based on the telephone interview administered to older focal children at Wave 2, but included content from the main respondent/ spouse interview not included at Wave 2.

Proxy interviews were required for main respondents who were deceased or too ill to be interviewed during Wave 3 and who did not have a spouse/partner to be interviewed. The proxy interview consisted of questions regarding the respondent's cause of death, conditions and disabilities, last employment, and living arrangements. Proxy interviews for main respondents were not necessary if there was a spouse or partner to be interviewed.

Several items in the main respondent/spouse NSFH Wave 3 instrument required respondents to provide an accounting of their lives since the time of their last interview, i.e. marital and cohabiting history since the time of the last interview, number of children born or adopted, and an account of who had moved in and out of the household. Two pretests were conducted to test the main respondent/spouse interview. After the pretest, debriefing sessions were held with pretest interviewers and further adjustments were made to the instrument. A pretest was conducted to test the focal child instrument and after the pretest, debriefing sessions were held with pretest interviewers and further modifications were made to the instrument.

3.2.3   Methods of Analysis

This section of the chapter will be devoted to discussing the methods of analysis that were used in this analysis. I will discuss multinomial logistic regression, which will be used to evaluate the degree of association between various independent variables and the probability of moving back home.

3.2.4   *Multinomial Logistic Regression*

For this project, I estimated multinomial logistic regression equations. I did not use the more popular regression technique, ordinary least squares (OLS) regression because my dependent variable is not continuous and unbounded; my dependent variable is multi-categorical. When the dependent variable is categorical, logistic regression should be employed. This method typically uses maximum likelihood (ML) estimation, which "are the values of the parameters that have the greatest likelihood of generating the observed sample of data if the assumptions of the model are true...the likelihood function tells us how likely it is that we would have observed the data that we did observe if these data were true population parameters" (Long and Freese 2003: 68).

Since my dependent variable has more than two categories, I use a form of logistic regression that has been extended beyond the analysis of a dichotomous variable to a variable with more than two categories (Menard 2002). I use multinomial logistic regression, the most frequently used nominal regression model. It is a regression model that generalizes logistic regression by allowing more than two discrete outcomes. It is a model that is used to predict the probabilities of the different outcomes of a categorically distributed dependent variable. Multinomial logistic regression is used when the dependent variable in question is nominal and consists of more than two categories. In the multinomial logit model, logits are formed from contrasts of non-redundant category pairs of the dependent variable. Each logit is then modeled in a separate equation.

The extension of the dichotomous logistic regression model to polytomous dependent variables is straightforward. One value of the dependent variable is designated as the reference category and set to zero, $(Y=h0)$, and takes on the role of the baseline or reference category, and the probability of membership in other categories is compared to the probability of membership in the reference or baseline category (Menard 2002). The coefficients are estimated in relation to the baseline category. Long and Freese note that "if the base outcome is not specified, the most frequent outcome in the estimation sample is chosen as the base" (2003: 229). In order to ensure that the category of comparison makes conceptual and theoretical sense in my analyses, I will set the base category in the estimated models.

Difficulty may arise from interpreting coefficients in terms of log odds, which may be easy to state but not so easily understood (Hamilton 1992). For example, if the independent variable is measuring whether or not an adult child moved back home had a coefficient of 1.00 for those adult children of a certain marital status (say, for instance, married), we could say that adult children who are married have a log odds of moving home that are 1.00 times higher as compared to those adult children who are unmarried. It is difficult to imagine what it means to have a 1.00 higher log odds. Because of the complexity associated with the interpretation of log odds, it is best to interpret the coefficients in terms of odds ratios by exponentiating the log odds. In multinomial logistic regression these exponentiated values are called relative risk ratios (rrr's). For a dummy variable the rrr is the odds of being in the dependent variable category of interest and not being in the base category, for the category of the independent dummy variable with a value of one versus the category with a value of zero. For ease of interpretation, I will calculate the rrr's for the multinomial logistic regression models that I will estimate.

Long and Freese (2003) tell us that we should be interested in looking at different combinations of the baseline to other category comparisons, beyond the category that we define as the baseline. By using the "listcoef" command, we can display all combinations of outcome categories without re-estimating the multinomial logit model in STATA. The "listcoef" command will be used in my analysis for this and other purposes.

3.2.5   Design Effects

Treiman (2009) tells us that the fact that national sample surveys are often based on multistage area probability samples creates a problem if the complex sampling design is not taken into consideration. The problem is that standard statistical packages (including STATA) assume that a survey was based on random sampling. If the survey was based on multistage probability sampling, the default assumption that the data are from a simple random sample tends to "understate the true extent of sampling error in the data. The reason for this is that when observations are clustered (drawn from a few selected sampling points), for many variables the within-cluster variance tends to be smaller than the variance across the population as a whole. This in turn implies that the between-cluster variance, i.e., the variance of the cluster means, which gives the standard error for clustered samples, is inflated relative to the variance of the same variable computed from a simple random sample drawn from the same population" (Treiman 2009: 207).

In many cases we see that the third stage of multistage probability samples are generally fairly homogenous with respect to various sociodemographic variables. The third and smallest stage of multistage samples normally have inhabitants with characteristics that are similar on a variety of levels such as education, age and race, and this is especially the case when comparing the third stage of multistage probability samples to the population of the entire country. As a result of this homogeneity, there is a smaller within-cluster variance among the variables, while the likelihood that the variance between clusters differs substantially. As such, we need to take into account the "variance among individuals in a cluster as well as the variance between clusters" (Treiman 2009: 207).

This is why survey estimation procedures are useful. STATA's survey estimation procedures are capable of handling multistage designs with more than two levels. Treiman (2009) further notes that in order to obtain correct estimates of standard errors for multistage samples, we need to use estimation procedures specifically designed for such samples. STATA provides a set of survey estimation commands to estimate standard errors for many common statistics, including means, proportions, OLS regression coefficients, logistic regression coefficients, and so forth.

These commands make it possible to take account of both clustering and stratification at each level of a multistage sample. According to Treiman, STATA requires that information regarding the properties of the data be set before entering the estimation commands. Once this is done, using STATA's "svyset" command, the estimation is carried out in the usual way except that the survey version of the estimation command is substituted for the non- survey version.

As Treiman has noted, few if any of the micro-level sample datasets we use in demography are simple random samples. A survey sample is almost never a true scale model of the population; if it were, this would mean that the response rates and coverage would be the same in every sub-group; the sample would thus be a "scale model" of the population. A survey sample is almost never a "scale model" as groups are often selected at different rates and often have different response rates, as is the case with the NSFH. Sampling weights adjust for different sampling rates, response rates, and coverage rates. Such adjustments enable the investigator to develop so-called "national" estimates from the sample that are accurate. A respondent's sampling weight may be interpreted as the number of persons in the population that he or she represents. For example, if a woman's sampling weight is 8000, then she represents 8,000 women in the population.

As previously stated the third wave of the NSFH consists of 9,230 men and women, based on an original national probability sample from Wave 1 of 13,007 For the NSFH, the sampling error measures the variation caused by interviewing 10,007 men and women in the NSFH instead of the 70 million men and women aged 18–34 and the 63 million men and women aged 35–96 in the entire population. It measures the variation of the estimated statistic over repeated samples of the same size. Theoretically, the sampling variance would be zero if the full population were observed. Because of the complex sample design of the NSFH, analysts should use weights in their analyses and use software that will compute "design based" estimates of sampling errors. Failure to use these weights and accurate variance estimates could well lead to biased or inaccurate findings and conclusions.

3.2.6 Dependent Variable

In this project, the dependent variable is constructed by recoding the information gathered from the following questions from the Focal Child interview on the NSFH:

1. Have you ever lived on your own, away from your parents' household, for 4 months or longer?
2. Did you ever move back home, other than for school vacations?

The categories of the dependent variable thus pertain to adult children who never moved out of the family home (failure to launch), moved out of the family home and then returned (previously launched), and moved out of the family home and did not return (successfully launched). The multinomial logistic model can be thought of as simultaneously estimating binary logits for all comparisons among the alternatives. For example, let launching status be a nominal outcome with the categories failure to launch (FTL), previously launched (PL) and successfully launched (SL). This dependent variable is suitable for a multinomial logistic regression model as already discussed.

The dependent variable in this analysis will be whether or not the individual has moved back in with the parents. The baseline category will be SL, or those that are successfully launched. This category includes those adult children who have moved out and lived on their own for 4 months or more and did not return home. This methodological approach is important for many reasons. The primary reason is that, as I have previously stated, many studies about parental happiness with the coresidence of adult children do not differentiate between children who have returned home and children who never left (Mitchell 1998). My study will be the first, to my knowledge, to differentiate between adult children who moved out of the home and then returned and adult children who never left the family home.

3.2.7 Independent Variables, Dependent Variables and Theoretical Approaches

The main independent variables include various standard demographic variables such as gender, education, race, socioeconomic status, and employment status. Separate regression equations were estimated for each theoretical perspective I used. Using the life course perspective, I will introduce the variables of parents' age, child's age, child's marital status, child's education level, and child's number of children. All of these variables relate to the life course, as the life course examines the timing of various events in an individual's life. The relationship between parents' position in the life course and the adult child's position in the life course is important, as I have demonstrated that parents at certain positions in the life course may be more or less likely to have adult children move back in with them, and the same can be said about adult children. The life course perspective is particularly useful because we can see the interplay between the lives of the parents and the life of the adult child.

The variables parent's age and child's age are simple continuous variables, asked as "respondent's age at time of interview." Child's marital status was recoded; current marital status was operationalized as either married (0) or not married (1). Child's education level was recoded as well; educational attainment was operationalized as "high school graduate" (1 = yes, 0 = no) and graduated from college/received a degree (1 = yes, 0 = no). Child's number of children is a continuous variable, asked as "how many children do you have?"

Using the family development framework, I examined the variables that related to the family structure into which the adult child will be moving back. I examined parents' marital/cohabitation status, number of siblings, parents' health and well being, and how well the adult child gets along with his/her parents (which includes questions asked of both the parents and the focal child).

Using economic theories of exchange, I examined variables of child's income, occupation and employment status, and other economic variables. Parents' marital status was recoded into married (1) and not married (0). Number of siblings is a continuous variable, ranging from 0 to 20 or more. Parents' health and well being is ascertained through the questions "Taking things all together, on a scale of 1–7, where 1 is very unhappy and seven is very happy, how would you say things are these days?" The next question, "Please tell me whether you strongly agree, agree, neither agree nor disagree, disagree, or strongly disagree with each of the following statements: On the whole, I am satisfied with myself." is the second question used to ascertain parents' health. Questions relating to how well the adult child gets along with parents were analyzed using the questions of "taking things all together, on a scale from 0 to 10, where 0 is really bad and 10 is absolutely perfect, how would you describe your relationship with your mother/father/step-parent?" Modeling the last equation after my prior research, I examined both variables that I have previously discussed as well as some that will have not yet been included in the regressions. Past research has focused on variables such as age, sex, race, and socioeconomic status of the adult child individually or in conjunction with one another. These basic demographic variables deserve examination despite the fact that they do not necessarily fit in neatly with one of the aforementioned theoretical frameworks.

In order to see which theoretical approach has the best explanatory power, I will compare the pseudo R^2 values of each theoretically specified model. Like the R^2 in ordinary least squares regression which measures the overall fit of the model, the pseudo R^2 value allows us to analyze how well the model fits the data. One limitation of logistic regression is that it does not have a goodness-of-fit measure; however, several proxies for the R^2 statistic are available. Because none of the pseudo R^2s support a straightforward explained variance interpretation, as does the true R^2, there is little agreement as to which pseudo R^2 is the best to use in analysis. However, the STATA command "fitstat" provides numerous goodness-of-fit statistics from which to choose, including McKelvey and Zavoina's R^2.

Wave 3 of the NSFH was separated into multiple datasets. I merged them into one dataset for this project; the dataset of the main respondent, the dataset of the focal child, and the dataset of the main respondent roster were combined. This was done in order to obtain all pertinent variables relating to theoretical approaches that I want to use in my analyses. The variables in each dataset were first sorted by case identification number (caseid) and then saved. Then I merged the datasets and then identified which cases matched. Out of a total of 9229 cases, 7277 matched. The cases that did not match were dropped from the merged dataset.

3.3 Sample Characteristics

3.3.1 Focal Children

The first group of variables that I will discuss measures the characteristics of the adult children. The variable, which was created by combining two previous variables, is recoded as "LaunchNew." This variable basically measures the adult child's launching status. The first category, never moved out (failure to launch), has a frequency of 179, or almost 11 % of the sample. The second category, moved out and returned (previously launched), has a frequency of 545 or about 33 % of the sample. The last and baseline category, moved out and did not return (successfully launched), has a frequency of 956 or about 57 % of the sample. The total sample numbers 1,680 and the majority of this sample, obviously, consists of those adult children who moved out of the family home and did not return.

For the focal child's age, the range was from 18 to 34, with almost all respondents being equally distributed at each age, with about 7 % at each age. This is true except at ages 18 and 34, which had about 1 % at each. The education variable has three categories, completed high school, enrolled in college or university, and received degree from college or university. About 91 % of the sample had obtained a high school degree, 66 % had enrolled in college or university, and 33 % had received a college degree. The annual income level was a simple continuous variable, ranging in value from 0 to 5,00,000. Those with incomes less than zero were dropped from the sample. Of the sample of focal children, 66 % were not married and 34 % were married. Regarding the "living with parents" variable, about 14 % said that living with their parents was going badly, and about 86 % said that it was going well. The question relating to the acceptability of adult children living with their parents shows that about 20 % believed that living with parents is not acceptable, while about 80 % agreed that it is acceptable to live with parents. The sex breakdown of the respondents was about 46 % male and 54 % female.

3.4 Conclusion

In this chapter I introduced the data and methods that I used in the analyses of this research project. The nature of the question I am investigating and the data that I am using necessitate the use of a multinomial logistic regression model for the analyses, as the dependent variable- launching status- is an unordered, nominal categorical dependent variable. I discussed the strengths and weaknesses of the dataset I have chosen to use as well as the methods that will be used in subsequent chapters of this book.

Chapter 4
Quantitative Results

Abstract In this chapter I discuss the results of the tests of my hypotheses focusing on models dealing with the life course and family development perspectives. Specifically, I discuss the results of the multinomial logistic regression analyses using the data obtained from Wave 3 of the NSFH. I have estimated two models with the Wave of data, as I have already mentioned; one model uses variables relating to the life course, and one model uses variables relating to family structure. Also in each model I used standard demographic variables as controls. I then provide descriptive results using data from the ACS which details topics such as age, sex, race, family and relationships, income and benefits, health insurance, education, veteran status, disabilities, work and journey to work, and expenses related to housing and housing occupancy.

Keywords Results • Statistics • Quantitative • Data • Regression

In this chapter I discuss the results of the tests of my hypotheses focusing on models dealing with the life course and family development perspectives. Specifically, I discuss the results of the multinomial logistic regression analyses using the data obtained from Wave 3 of the NSFH. I have estimated two models with the Wave of data, as I have already mentioned; one model uses variables relating to the life course, and one model uses variables relating to family structure. Also in each model I used standard demographic variables as controls.

First I discuss my hypotheses, and then begin the analysis of the NSFH data by presenting and discussing several descriptive statistics that provide some perspective and overall legitimacy for the analyses of this book. I hope that the use of these figures and tables clarifies the data and the way that I use these data to study the phenomenon of previously launched adults in the United States.

© Springer International Publishing Switzerland 2016
D.N. Farris, *Boomerang Kids: The Demography of Previously Launched Adults*,
SpringerBriefs in Population Studies, DOI 10.1007/978-3-319-31227-9_4

4.1 Hypotheses

Prior literature related to previously launched adults reports mixed and often conflicting results. Utilizing the life course perspective, we can see various issues that impact the prevalence of adult children moving back in with their parents. Depending on the parents' position in the life course, their adult children may be more or less likely to be living back at home with them. We see that middle-aged parents with young adult children may have children living with them as a result of "the continued dependence of children on their parents" (Aquilino 1990: 406). Conversely, parents who are elderly may coreside with older adult children owing to their dependence on them. However, we have seen that this is not as likely an occurrence as the former. Furthermore, the life course perspective offers a view that focuses on the interdependence of the lives of the adult children and their parents.

From an economic viewpoint and using an exchange theory framework, it would appear to be more likely that adult children will live with their parents as a result of economic vulnerability and other needs based considerations. We have consistently seen that living back at home tends to be more advantageous for a young adult child than for the parent with whom they are residing, and it is likely that adult children have assessed the costs and benefits of living back at home and have chosen this arrangement due to the benefits they will receive as a result.

Thus, I hypothesized that adult children with younger parents will be more likely to live at home than adult children with older parents. Likewise, I hypothesized that younger adult children will be more likely to live at home than older adult children. Additionally, it is likely that the life course trajectory of the adult child will have an impact on whether s/he moves back home. Adult children who are married are less likely to return home; however there appears to be a racial differential in these findings in that this is more evident among non-Hispanic whites (White 1994). Thus, I hypothesized that adult children who are married will be less likely to live at home, as will adult children who have children.

Some previous literature states that those with lower socioeconomic status may be more likely to move back home. This conclusion is interesting and deserves closer scrutiny. Adult children with a low individual socioeconomic status may very well be likely to move back home. I found this result with many of the respondents in my qualitative study. Among my respondents, a majority of those interviewed reported having no job, a high student loan debt, and no other promising alternatives to moving back in with their parents. These are two of the three main contributing factors of one's socioeconomic status (income and occupation) and surely indicate a low socioeconomic status. However, these individuals all had high levels of education; all of my respondents graduated from 4 year accredited top tier, second tier, or Ivy League universities. This mismatch on dimensions of social class leads to what sociologists refer to as status inconsistency. Additionally, while these respondents may have had a low personal socioeconomic status, their parents had quite high socioeconomic statuses; most respondents reported that their parents were in the upper-middle to upper class. Their parents had the resources to allow their children to move back in with them, and bear the brunt of having another mouth to feed, to shelter, and to pay for in miscellaneous ways.

Likewise, Aquilino (1990) argues that the family's ability to house and support adult children may influence the timing of home leaving, and I would extend this to include home returning. Other researchers, namely, Goldscheider and DeVanzo (1985) have drawn similar conclusions regarding family income and the likelihood of coresidence. It makes sense then that those with low individual socioeconomic statuses would be likely to move back in with parents. I hold that socioeconomic status plays an important role on whether or not a child will be able to move back in with the family. Some families may simply not have enough room for an adult child to move back home, and adult children who have children of their own will make an already crowded situation even more complicated. I hypothesize that the lower the incomes of adult children, the more likely they will be to live at home.

Additionally, based on previous research, I hypothesized that men will be more likely to be living in the family home than women. This may appear to be inconsistent with so-called common sense in that it is often thought that men are expected to acquire their independence and start a life and family of their own earlier than women. However, as I have already noted, previous research shows that men in fact are more likely to be living at home than women, and frequently to the detriment to their parents' happiness. Previous research notes that women are more likely to leave the parental home earlier than men and are also less likely to return home. White (1994) for instance has argued that this is due to women's earlier age at marriage, although this factor may not be as salient in the current time of delayed age at marriage and childbearing among young women.

Prior research has shown that males are more likely than females to believe that parents have an obligation to house their children and are less likely to feel that children should be obligated to pay back their parents in return (White 1994). Other theories of the family describe the differential in terms of the effects of daughters living back at home on the parent-child relationship. White (1994) suggests that girls who stay in or return to the family home may be more supervised than boys and will be more expected than boys to help out with more housework.

I hypothesized that the education level of the child will have a significant effect on the likelihood of living back at home. I was not able to test this hypothesis in my previous research because all my respondents came from a variety of collegiate backgrounds, but all had a college education. I hypothesized that those with a degree will be less likely to be living at home than those without a degree.

Additional variables relating to family structure are also important to include in my research. Prior research shows that adult children with many siblings or whose parents are divorced, separated or remarried are less likely to return home (Aquilino 1990; White 1994; Mitchell 1998). Lack of cohesion in families may be found in stepfamilies and this may well decrease the likelihood of an adult child moving back home; thus I hypothesize that adult children with married parents will be more likely to live at home. This research also shows that families that experience conflict or adult children who do not get along with one of their parents will be unlikely to move back home; thus I hypothesized that that adult children who get along well with their parents will be more likely to move back or continue to live at home than those who do not get along well with their parents. Also, based on previous research, I hypothesized that adult children with more brothers and sisters will be less likely to live at home.

Other features of the family structure perspective are the health and well being of the parents of the adult children. As previously stated, many adult children may move back in with their parents as a result of the deteriorating health of the parents. Although I do not hold that this will be the main motivating factor leading adult children to move back in with their parents, I do believe that parents who are in poorer health will be more likely to have adult children living at home with them. That is, parents who report that things are not "good these days" and that they are dissatisfied with themselves will be more likely to have adult children living at home.

I suspected that race/ethnicity will also be related to the risk of moving back home with parents. I hold that that certain groups may view moving back home or more specifically, delaying the transition of moving out of the parental home, as being more acceptable and normative that would be the case with other groups. Culturally, on average certain racial groups do not see living at home, or returning home after leaving, as being non-normative. A core element of deeply rooted values of Hispanic culture is familism (Landale and Oropesa 2007). Living in the family home until the time of marriage, especially for females, is very common. Familism is the idea that a collective orientation is more important than an individual orientation and implies that "family roles are highly valued and family members are oriented more toward the needs of the family unit than to their individual desires" (Landale and Oropesa 2007: 396). It seems that owing to familism, Hispanic adult children may be more likely to let their parents move in with them in later life. Following this pattern I expected to find that Hispanics will be more likely to be living with their parents than non-Hispanic whites. Other studies show that African-Americans and Asians are also less likely to be home leavers, which is also attributable to the familism theory just delineated with respect to Hispanics. Unfortunately, the Wave 3 data do not provide the detailed data enabling me to determine race/ethnic identification of the respondents.

Despite the fact that I will be unable to test whether there is a statistical relationship between race/ethnic identification and launching status of young adults, I will be able to use descriptive data from the American Community Survey to examine some of the characteristics of persons living and not living at home, one of which will be race/ethnic identification.

4.2 Analyses

As already discussed in this chapter, the main concerns of interest in this book pertain to home leaving and returning. The analyses in this chapter use a variety of independent variables of interest in my examination of home leaving and returning.

As previously stated, the main objective of the analyses is to determine the statistically influential factors (X variables) that lead to or detract from the likelihood of an adult child moving out of the parental home and then returning. The dependent variable is comprised of three possible outcomes, namely, never moved out of the family home, moved out and then returned to the family home, and moved out and did not return to the family home. The base category will be moved out and did not return to the family home; persons in this category will be referred to as "successfully launched adults." Before turning to the testing of my hypotheses, I first describe the data that will be included in the models.

4.3 Descriptive Results

In this section of the chapter I provide descriptive results of the independent and dependent variables measured with data. The first point to be mentioned is that this sample was restricted to those main respondents and their corresponding focal children. Thus, the sample size was 1,382 persons. While there are a total of 7,433 cases in the entire sample, there are almost 6,000 missing values on some of the variables. In order to maintain a consistent number of cases, I restricted my analyses in the models to those with no missing values. Since the variable measuring the launching status of the young adults is an unordered categorical variable, the minimum value is one and the maximum value is three. I next present in Table 4.1 similar descriptive statistics for the independent variables and the variables to be used as controls.

Since some of the variables are dummy variables, their minimum values are zero and maximum values are one. About 33 % of the sample holds a degree or certificate. The mean age of the children is 25 and the mean age of the parents is 57. About 65% of the sample is not married. Number of children is a continuous variable and ranges from zero to five, with a mean of .68 children. Income has been recoded into four categories; one ($0–30,000 annual income), two ($30,001–65,000 annual income), three ($65,001–100,000 annual income) and four ($100,001 and higher annual income).

Table 4.1 Descriptive statistics for life course model, Wave 3

Independent variables	Minimum	Maximum	Mean	Standard deviation
Life course variables				
Parent's age	31	100	57.789	11.998
Child's age	18	34	25.79	4.440
Child's marital status	0	1	.6598	.4738
Child's education level (Degree)	0	1	.3335	.4716
Child's number of children	0	5	.6838	1.0187
Control variables				
Sex	0	1	.4624	.4987
Income	1	4	1.324	.57808

Table 4.2 Descriptive statistics for family development model, Wave 3

Independent variables	Minimum	Maximum	Mean	Standard deviation
Family development framework variables				
Parent's marital status	0	1	.8228	.3818
Child's number of siblings	0	20	2.648	2.1303
Parent's health/well being (1)	1	7	5.673	1.204
Parent's health/well being(2)	1	5	1.954	.7598
Get along (Mom)	0	10	8.085	1.702
Get along (Dad)	0	10	6.699	2.716
Control variables				
Sex	0	1	.4624	.4987
Income	1	4	1.324	.5780
Age	18	34	25.79	4.440

The second model pertains to variables relating to family development and structure. Table 4.2 presents the descriptive results for this model.

Table 4.2 shows that most of the parents are married and that the average number of siblings of the focal child is 2.6. Assessing how "things are these days," parents reported a mean of 5.6, indicating a fairly high level of happiness. When asked about self-satisfaction, parents reported a mean of 1.95, meaning they strongly agree that they are satisfied with themselves. On a scale of one to ten, focal children rated their relationships with their mothers very highly, with a mean of 8.1. Focal children rated their relationships with their fathers slightly lower, with a mean of 6.7.

4.4   Multinomial Logistic Regression Results

In this section I report the results of the multinomial logistic regression using the aforementioned independent variables. The results are shown in separate tables for each of four models. The multinomial regression results are reported with relative risk ratios. As discussed previously, relative risk ratios (rrr's) are the exponentiated values of the multinomial logistic regression coefficients; these enable the multiplicative interpretation of the risk of being in a previously launched adult category as opposed to the reference category of "successfully launched." Although some of the variables were not associated with increasing the risk of being a "failure to launch" or a "previously launched adult," some were shown to be associated with an increased or decreased risk of being in one of these categories. I now discuss the results in Table 4.3.

As shown in the above table, only one of the X variables relating to the life course was shown to not have any significant association with launching status for

Table 4.3 Multinomial logistic regression results (Odds Ratios) without control variables, life course variables Wave 3

Life course variables	Odds ratios
Group 1 (Failure to launch)	
Parent's age	1.0267
Child's age	.89183***
Child's marital status	14.0705***
Child's education (Degree)	.58646*
Child's number children	.60445**
Group 2 (Previously launched)	
Parent's age	1.0074
Child's age	1.1444***
Child's marital status	1.4813**
Child's education (Degree)	.88654
Child's number children	.98092

N = 1382
LR Chi^2 = 302.67
Prob > Chi^2 = 0.000
Pseudo R^2 = 0.1079
* p > 0.05 ** p > 0.01 *** p > 0.001

the first category. The age of the parent was not significantly associated with having never moved out of the family home. In the second model, we see that the age of the parent, education of the child, and number of children the child had were not significantly associated with moving out of the family home and then returning.

For the life course variables in the category "failure to launch," child's age, child's marital status, child's education, and child's number of children were significantly associated with the risk of being a "failure to launch" child. Child's age had a relative risk ratio of .8918, which may be interpreted as follows: The value of .8918 means that each change in a value on the age category of the children multiplies the risk by a factor of .8918 of being a failure to launch versus a successfully launched young adult. That is, the risk is decreased by about 10.8 %. This variable is also significant in the model for previously launched adults. In the previously launched adults model, the relative risk ratio value is 1.144. This value means that each change in a value on the age category of the child multiplies the risk by a factor of 1.144 of being a previously launched. That is, the risk is increased by about 14.4 %. In the failure to launch model, the relative risk ratio is significant at the p>0.001 level and in the previously launched model the relative risk ratio is significant at the p>0.001 level.

In the model for failure to launch, child's marital status has a relative risk ratio of 14.07. This means that compared to married individuals, unmarried adult children have a risk that is multiplied by a factor of 14 of being a failure to launch; that is, their risk is increased by 1307.1 %. This relative risk ratio is significant at the p>0.001 level. In the model for previously launched adults, the variable for marital status has a relative risk ratio of 1.48. This means that compared to married individuals, unmarried individuals multiply the risk by a factor of 1.48 of being a previously launched versus a successfully launched adult; that is, the risk is increased by about 48.1 %. This relative risk ratio is significant at the p>0.01 level.

In the failure to launch model, the variable for education has a relative risk ratio of .586. This means that compared to those without a degree, those with a degree have a risk for being a failure to launch that is multiplied by a factor of .59; that is, the risk is decreased by 41.4 %. This relative risk ratio is significant at the p>0.05 level. In the previously launched model the variable for education has a relative risk ratio of .89. This means that compared to those without a degree, those with a degree have a risk of being a previously launched adult that is multiplied by a risk factor of .89; that is, the risk is decreased by 11.3 %; however this relative risk ratio is not significant.

In the failure to launch model, the variable for child's number of children has a relative risk ratio of .60. This means that for every increase in the number of children an adult child has, the risk of being a failure to launch child is multiplied by a factor of .60; that is, the risk is decreased by 39.6 %. This relative risk ratio is significant at the p>0.01 level of significance. In the model for previously launched, the variable for child's number of children has a relative risk ratio of .98. However, this relative risk ratio is not significant.

I next now turn to a discussion of the statistical model using the family development framework and various family related variables. Table 4.4 presents these results.

As shown in the table, far fewer variables related to the child's family structure and family development are significantly associated with launching status. Parent's

Table 4.4 Multinomial logistic regression results (Odds ratios) without control variables, family development variables Wave 3

Family development variables	Odds ratios
Group 1 (Failure to launch)	
Parent's marital	.69219
Number siblings	1.03221
Parent's health (1)	.86317
Parent's health (2)	.76090*
Get along (Mom)	.95367
Get along (Dad)	1.05869
Group 2 (Previously Launched)	
Parent's marital	.99025
Number siblings	1.09813**
Parent's health (1)	.89131*
Parent's health (2)	.87263
Get along (Mom)	.99989
Get along (Dad)	.93508*

N = 1382
LR Chi² = 23.66
Prob > Chi² = 0.0226
Pseudo R² = 0.0124
* p > 0.05 ** p > 0.01 *** p > 0.001

marital status, number of brothers and sisters, parent's health and well being (1), how well the adult child gets along with the mother, and how well the adult child gets along with the father are not significant predictors of a child being a failure to launch. Likewise, parent's marital status, parent's health and well being (2), and how well the adult child gets along with the mother, are not significant predictors of whether the child will be previously launched.

However, in the first analysis, the variable for parent's health and well-being (2) does have a significant effect on launching status. In the second analysis, number of siblings, parent's health and well being (1), and how well the adult child gets along with the father are significant predictors of launching status. The relative risk ratio for parent's health and well-being (2) is .76. This means that for every unit increase in the variable (as a parent feels less satisfied with themselves), the risk of a child being a failure to launch is decreased by 13.7 %. This relative risk ratio is significant at $p > 0.05$.

The variable for number of siblings has a relative risk ratio of 1.1. This means that for every increase in the number of siblings an adult child has, the risk of being a previously launched adult is increased by 9.8 %, and this relative risk ratio is statistically significant. The variable for parent's health and well-being (1) has a relative risk ratio of .89 meaning that for every unit increase in the variable (as a parent is more happy with things these days), the risk of being a previously launched adult is decreased by 10.9 %. This relative risk ratio also is significant. The relative risk ratio for the variable of how well the adult child gets along with the father is .94. This means that for every unit increase on the variable (as the child gets along better with the father), the risk of being a previously launched adult is decreased by 6.5 %, and this effect too is significant.

I now turn to a more detailed discussion of the models by analyzing them while including the relevant control variables of sex and income. Table 4.5 shows the results of the analysis using the life course variables and the control variables.

The model focusing on life course variables plus the controls with regard to failure to launch shows that child's age, child's marital status, child's number of children, child's sex, and income were all significantly associated with the risk of being a failure to launch child. Child's age had a relative risk ratio of .89 meaning that when the controls are introduced the risk is decreased by about 11.7 %. This variable is also significant but in the opposite direction in the model for previously launched adults.

In the model for failure to launch, the variable of child's marital status has a relative risk ratio of 11.1 indicating a very strong positive effect of marital status. In the model for previously launched adults, the marital status variable is also positive but not as strong as in the previous model. In the failure to launch model, the variable for child's number of children has a relative risk ratio of .67. The greater the number of children, the less the risk.

In the failure to launch model, the child's sex has a relative risk ratio of 1.71. This means that compared to women, men have a greater risk of being a failure to launch versus being successfully launched. In the previously launched model, males are less likely than females to be previously launched. The variable for income is only

Table 4.5 Multinomial
logistic regression results
(Odds ratios) with control
variables, life course
variables Wave 3

Life course variables	Odds ratios
Group 1 (Failure to Launch)	
Parent's age	1.02866
Child's age	.89338**
Child's marital Status	11.1150***
Child's education (Degree)	.79185
Child's number Children	.67824*
Sex	1.70788**
Income	.44172**
Group 2 (Previously Launched)	
Parent's age	1.0082
Child's age	1.1467***
Child's marital status	1.4421**
Child's education (Degree)	.86633
Child's number children	.96639
Sex	.73763**
Income	1.0052

N = 1382
LR Chi^2 = 282.85
Prob > Chi^2 = 0.000
Pseudo R^2 = 0.1114
* p > 0.05 ** p > 0.01 *** p > 0.001

significant in the model for failure to launch. The multinomial logistic regression
models that analyze the relationship between the life course variables, the control
variables, and launching status provide some interesting results. My hypothesis
regarding parent's age was not supported. My hypothesis regarding child's age was
supported and age was proven to be significantly associated with launching status in
the failure to launch model.

However, in the previously launched model, contrary to my hypothesis, older
adults were more likely to move back in with their parents and this finding was
significant. Thus, my hypothesis was confirmed for only one group of adult
children.

I hypothesized that both adult children who were married and those with children
would be less likely to live at home. My hypothesis for marital status was supported
and significant in both models; however my hypothesis for number of children was
only significant in the model for failure to launch. My hypothesis for education was
also supported; however the results were not significant. My hypothesis regarding
sex was interesting in that males were shown to be more likely to be living at home
than females, but this was only the case for those who were failures to launch. My
hypothesis that adult children with higher incomes would be less likely to move
back home was supported for failure to launch adults, but not supported for previously launched adults. However, with the failure to launch model this variable was
significant and in the previously launched model it was not significant.

Table 4.6 Multinomial logistic regression results (Odds ratios) with control variables, family development variables Wave 3

Family development variables	Odds ratios
Group 1 (Failure to launch)	
Parent's marital	.6806737
Number siblings	1.032243
Parent's health (1)	.8986739
Parent's health (2)	.799200
Get along (Mom)	.9511848
Get along (Dad)	1.049486
Sex	2.349628***
Income	.229070**
Age	.8309831***
Group 2 (Previously launched)	
Parent's marital	.7317886
Number siblings	1.077751*
Parent's health (1)	.8085982 **
Parent's health (2)	.8503174
Get along (Mom)	1.013673
Get along (Dad)	.9386832*
Sex	.7414978 *
Income	.8816769
Age	1.140864***

N = 1382
LR Chi^2 = 199.13
Prob > Chi^2 = 0.000
Pseudo R^2 = 0.1151
*p > 0.05 ** p > 0.01 *** p > 0.001

I now turn to a discussion of the results of the statistical model using the family development framework and various family related variables. Table 4.6 shows these results.

As depicted in the table, several variables related to family development were not shown to have any significant association with launching status. In the model for failure to launch, parent's marital status, number of siblings, parent's health, how well the child gets along with the mother, and how well the child gets along with the father were all shown to not have any significant association with launching status. However, in the model for previously launching status, only parent's marital status, the second variable relating to parent's health and well being, and how well the adult child gets along with their mother and income were not significantly associated with launching status.

For the failure to launch category, the only variables that were significantly associated with launching status were sex, income, and age, all of which were used as control variables in the models. For the previously launched category, number of siblings, parent's health, how well the adult child gets along with their father, sex, and age were significantly associated with launching status.

The relative risk ratio for number of siblings is 1.1 meaning that the greater the number of siblings, the greater the risk of being a previously launched adult. This finding is inconsistent with my hypothesis that adult children would be less likely to live at home if they had more siblings. The relative risk ratio for parent's health is .81. The healthier the parent, the less the risk of being a previously launched adult. This finding is consistent with my hypothesis.

The relative risk ratio for how well the adult child gets along with his/her father is .94, indicating that this variable has a slightly negative risk of being a previously launched adult. This result is contrary to my hypothesis, in which I had predicted that adult children would be more likely to live at home if they got along well with their parents.

Some of my hypotheses relating to the family development framework and family structure were supported, but others were not. However many of the variables did not turn out to be significant with the addition of the control variables. Prior to the addition of control variables in the models, parent's health and well-being was shown to be significantly associated with launching status, namely the launching status of failure to launch; however as the parent was more dissatisfied with themselves they are less likely to have an adult child living at home, which was contrary to my hypothesis. For previously launched adults, the hypothesis relating to number of siblings was significantly associated with previously launched adults launching status, which also was inconsistent with my expectations. Additionally, parent's health and well being (1) was proven to be significantly related to launching status and in the direction predicted. How well the adult child got along with the father was also significant, albeit in a direction opposite to that expected.

I found many of these findings surprising, especially the fact that a majority of the family structure and family development variables were not significantly associated with the launching status of an adult child. As shown in my review of the literature, family development has focused on the characteristics of families over the period of their existence and also on the content and timing of past events in individual histories and how these events affect present interaction patterns among family members (Aldous 1978). I began this project expecting that the different variables relating to the life course perspective would be very important and certainly have a significant impact on launching status. However, I had also suspected that the family development framework variables would be quite significant as well. Despite the fact that with recent changes in the composition of marriage and families leading to a change in the timing and sequencing of events in the family, I had still hypothesized that variables relating to the family would significantly impact the launching status of young adults; clearly, my hypotheses were not supported with the data.

4.5 Discussion

In the first part of this chapter I have displayed and discussed the results of the series of models examining various predictors of the launching status of adults. The analyses were conducted with two separate models; one that focused on life course variables and one that focused on family development and family structure variables.

However, some of my hypotheses were not confirmed, most especially those related to the various family development and family structure variables. I was surprised that the results indicated that very few of the family related variables were significant predictors of launching status because I had anticipated that the family structure variables would in fact be very significant predictors. I think that this finding is very interesting and deserves more attention in future research relating to adults who move back in with their parents. Unfortunately, the only dataset that specifically addresses the questions of adult children moving back in with their parents is the one I used in this book.

I next will describe the data from the American Community Survey and will focus in particular on some of the descriptive statistics of families and living arrangements in the more recent year of 2009. This dataset does not contain detailed enough data to permit me to retest the hypotheses I tested with the NSFH data. But there are sufficient enough data in the ACS to enable me to describe some of the characteristics of families and family relationships that will help provide more information about the young adults who are the subject of this book. I am able to provide from the ACS good descriptions of families and their living arrangements, but the ACS does not have the detailed information needed to test and evaluate my hypotheses. Despite this shortcoming, its data are valuable for providing descriptive information. Therefore in this section I first describe in some detail the ACS, its rationale and its content. Then I turn to a fuller discussion regarding the reasoning for including the descriptive statistics obtained from the ACS. I conclude with a presentation of the descriptive data from the ACS about families and living arrangements.

4.6 The American Community Survey

4.6.1 Introduction

According to the United States Census Bureau,[1] the ACS is an ongoing survey that provides data and is the "cornerstone of the U.S. Census Bureau's effort to keep pace with the nation's ever increasing demands for timely and relevant data about population and housing characteristics" (ACS Design Methodology Foreword: 1). The ACS was introduced to take the place of the long form questionnaire of the

---

[1] All information in this section obtained from http://www.census.gov/acs/www/

decennial census, which provided detailed data about the American population once every 10 years. Since the ACS is an annual survey, detailed data are now provided annually, not decennially.

The ACS details topics such as age, sex, race, family and relationships, income and benefits, health insurance, education, veteran status, disabilities, work and journey to work, and expenses related to housing and housing occupancy. The ACS utilizes a series of monthly samples to produce annually updated data for the areas formerly sampled only in the decennial census long-form sample; the ACS is vital to economic development and is an improvement over the long form questionnaire of the decennial census because it provides small-area information annually instead of only once a decade. Officials argue that the data obtained from the ACS are utilized to administer federal and state programs and note that the ACS has long lasting value for policy and decision making across all levels of government and private sectors.

4.6.2 Methodology

The traditional cross sectional model of the decennial U.S. Census involved observations of a population made at home at one point in time. In contrast to the cross sectional method of obtaining information about the populations, the longitudinal and continuous measurement of the detailed information on the characteristics of population and housing is available via the ACS. In the early 1990s, data users demanded current and nationally consistent data, leading the federal government policymakers to consider the feasibility of implementing a survey like the ACS. Rather than collecting data about a subset of the population once every 10 years via the long form instrument of the decennial census, the ACS would allow researchers to gather information on social, economic, and housing data continuously throughout the decade. The benefits of such a survey were many; the Census Bureau would be able to provide current data as well as the anticipated decennial census benefits in cost savings, planning, improved census coverage and more efficient operations. This information led the Census Bureau to plan the implementation of the ACS.

The designers of the ACS decided that data would be "collected continuously via the use of independent monthly samples...[and] three modes of data collection would be used: a primary mail survey to ensure cost efficiency, as well as telephone and personal visit non-response follow-up methods" (ACS Design Methodology Chap. 2).

Reports found that the data collected met basic Census Bureau standards and provided a reasonable alternative to the decennial census long- form sample. Other reports confirmed the usability and reliability of the ACS estimates and found that the Census long-form estimates and the ACS estimates were comparable.

Full implementation began in 2005 and population and housing profiles became available in the summer of 2006 and have been available every year subsequently for specific geographic areas with populations of 65,000 or more. Three- year period estimates reflect the combined data from the 2005 to 2007 ACS and were available in late 2008. Five-year period estimates were available in 2010. Beginning in 2010 and every year thereafter, the nation now has a 5-year period estimate available as an alternative to the decennial census long form sample; this serves as a community information resource that shows change over time.

In order to develop and produce detailed demographic, housing, social and economic data every year, the ACS attempts to minimize content changes in order to ensure reliability. According to the ACS Design Methodology (2010a), "the Census Bureau classifies all living quarters as either housing units or group quarters facilities. A housing unit is a house, apartment, and group of rooms or a single room. Group quarters facilities are living quarters owned and managed by an entity or organization that provides housing or services for the residents" (Chapter 6:1). Rules regarding who is eligible to be interviewed are defined in relation to residency status. Current residents are eligible to be interviewed and individuals are considered to be current residents if they are living in a residence at the time of the interview. This excludes those who are only staying there for a short period of time (less than two consecutive months). Residency for the group quarters facilities is determined by a de factor rule- all people staying in the group quarters facility when the roster of residents is made and sampled are eligible to be interviewed, regardless of the length of stay (ACS Design Methodology Chap. 6).

I obtained the data that I utilized for descriptive analysis from IPUMS-USA. IPUMS-USA contains harmonized data on people in the United States Census and the ACS from 1850 to present. I requested access to the 2009 ACS sample survey and included the variables for household and person records. These variables are state, person number, relationship to household head, age, sex, marital status, race and educational attainment.

4.7 Descriptive Statistics from the ACS on Families and Living Arrangements

I now present some descriptive statistics that detail the current situation of adult child/parent coresidence in the United States. As previously stated, these are data collected from the most recent ACS, which was in 2009. The sample I obtained has about 3 million observations. However, after restricting the sample to only the 18–34 year old children of the heads of the household, I was left with a sample of slightly more than 182,000. Table 4.7 is a frequency tabulation of the children by age and sex.

The majority of the young adults who are living at home are in the 18–24 age range. This is somewhat similar to the descriptive statistics obtained using the NSFH data; the average age for the children in those data was about 25. With a total of 182,486 young adults living at home who are between the ages of 18–34, this equates to slightly more than 15 % of the entire sample obtained from the ACS. After

Table 4.7 Living arrangements by age 18–34 and sex 2009 American community survey

Age	Male	Female
18	16,079	14,088
19	12,534	10,736
20	10,688	9,245
21	9,388	7,614
22	8,074	6,900
23	7,380	6,100
24	6,176	4,962
25	5,061	4,136
26	4,503	3,356
27	3,838	2,992
28	3,341	2,532
29	2,871	2,192
30	2,560	1,986
31	2,081	1,649
32	2,032	1,492
33	1,705	1,309
34	1,656	1,230
Total	**99,967**	**82,519**

age 24, the number of young adults living with their parents drops off slightly and continues to decline up until age 34. Obviously the largest number of young adults living at home are those who are 18 years old; this may well be because they have just turned 18 but have not yet graduated from high school.

Table 4.7 also shows that at all ages males outnumber females among those who live at home. This is s what I had hypothesized would be the case in my original analysis of the NSFH data. Similar to the original breakdown by age, a majority of young adults who are living at home are between the ages of 18 and 20. The numbers of young adults living at home continue to decline for both sexes as the young adults get older. Next, I analyze the racial identification of young adults who live at home (see Table 4.8).

Interestingly, the majority of the sample of young adults living at home is comprised of young adults who identify as white. This is likely because in the original sample, people who identified as white made up almost 80 % of the sample. The next largest group is comprised of those who identify as black. The third largest group is comprised of those who identify as other, which is a category that I created to include American Indian or Alaska Natives, other race, two major races and three or more major races. Lastly, those who identify as Asian make up the smallest portion of the sample, which includes those who identify as Chinese, Japanese, or Other Asian or Pacific Islanders. Another way to analyze the racial data is to examine the racial distribution by age; does the racial distribution vary by age? These results are shown in Table 4.8 as well, which indicates a pattern that is consistent with the aforementioned results.

The largest range is for those who identify as either White or Black but clearly the difference between the percentages at each age is fairly negligible. We see that

Table 4.8 Living arrangements by age and racial identification, 2009 American community survey

Age	White (%)	Black (%)	Asian (%)	Other (%)
18	22,512 (74.62)	3,428 (11.36)	1,242 (4.12)	2,985 (9.89)
19	17,072 (73.36)	2,767 (11.89)	1,045 (4.49)	2,386 (10.25
20	14,547 (72.98)	2,445 (12.27)	964 (4.84)	1,977 (9.92)
21	12,420 (73.05)	2,024 (11.90)	912 (5.36)	1,646 (9.68)
22	10,963 (73.21)	1,659 (11.08)	856 (5.72)	1,496 (9.99)
23	9,911 (73.52)	1,545 (11.46)	813 (6.03)	1,211 (8.98)
24	7,953 (71.40)	1,296 (11.64)	780 (7.00)	1,109 (9.96)
25	6,371 (69.27)	1,213 (13.19)	708 (7.70)	905 (9.84)
26	5,423 (69.00)	1,037 (13.20	602 (7.66)	797 (10.14)
27	4,721 (69.12)	917 (13.43)	510 (7.47)	682 (9.99)
28	3,991 (67.96	835 (14.22)	434 (7.39	613 (10.44)
29	3,414 (67.43)	739 (14.60)	388 (7.66)	522 (10.31)
30	3,024 (66.52)	723 (15.90)	347 (7.63)	452 (9.94)
31	2,567 (68.82)	538 (14.47)	261 (7.18)	364 (10.27)
32	2,399 (69.11)	510 (15.83)	253 (6.34)	362 (8.73)
33	2,083 (67.98)	477 (16.01)	191 (6.44)	261 (9.56)
34	1,962 (71.97)	562 (12.39)	186 (5.75)	276 (9.89)
Total	131,333	22,615	10,492	18,046

at each age, the distribution by race is roughly the same. Next I will examine data on Hispanic and non-Hispanic identification by the age of young adults living at home. Table 4.9 details the results.

The majority of the young adults who live at home do not identify as Hispanic. As depicted by the table, substantially less young adults who live at home identify as Hispanic at all ages. This is perhaps the case because in the original full ACS sample, a large percentage of respondents identified as non-Hispanic (about 86 %). A much smaller percentage of the original sample identified as Mexican, Puerto Rican, Cuban, or Other. The percentage that identified as Mexican, Puerto Rican, Cuban, or other was about 14 %. Much like the table depicting the percentage racial breakdown by age, the percentage Hispanic identification by age varies a very small amount. In this case, the amount of variation is even less than the range for the racial breakdown.

In the table above, the percentage of those who identified as Hispanic ranges from about 16 to 19 %. For those who identify as non-Hispanic, the percentage ranges from about 80 to 82 %. Unfortunately, due to data constrictions, I cannot make any comparisons between these descriptive results regarding race and Hispanic identification and the descriptive results from the NSFH because I was unable to analyze race and Hispanic identification using those data.

However, I have a strong feeling that if I had been able to obtain descriptive statistics regarding racial and Hispanic identification using the NSFH data, the breakdown by race would produce similar results. Lastly, I analyze the education levels of young adults living at home by age. Table 4.10 details these results.

Table 4.9 Living arrangements by age and hispanic identification, 2009 American community survey

Age	Hispanic (%)	Not hispanic (%)
18	5,360 (17.77)	24,807 (82.23)
19	4,300 (18.48)	18,970 (81.52)
20	3,621 (18.17)	16,312 (81.83)
21	3,099 (18.23)	13,903 (81.77)
22	2,724 (18.19)	12,250 (81.81)
23	2,359 (17.50)	11,121 (82.50)
24	2,017 (18.59)	9,067 (81.41)
25	1,659 (18.04)	7,538 (81.96)
26	1,456 (18.53)	6,403 (81.47)
27	1,329 (19.46)	5,501 (80.54)
28	1,163 (19.80)	4,710 (80.20)
29	950 (18.76)	4,113 (81.24)
30	845 (18.59)	3,701 (81.41)
31	694 (18.61)	3,036 (81.39)
32	686 (19.47)	2,828 (80.53)
33	542 (17.98)	2,472 (82.02)
34	457 (15.84)	2,429 (81.74)
Total	**33,315**	**149,171**

Table 4.10 Living arrangements by age and education, 2009 American community survey

Age	< High school	High school	Some college	College	> College
18	11,889	16,712	1,566	0	0
19	2,782	13,268	7,184	36	0
20	1,651	9,220	8,936	118	8
21	1,269	7,289	7,835	591	18
22	1,003	5,749	5,774	2,381	67
23	926	4,845	4,458	3,077	174
24	816	4,064	3,288	2,691	279
25	719	3,418	2,668	2,050	342
26	674	3,036	2,168	1,631	350
27	644	2,751	1,699	1,401	335
28	592	2,443	1,453	1,093	292
29	540	2,120	1,297	834	272
30	490	2,011	1,109	685	251
31	419	1,599	913	609	190
32	411	1,581	813	533	186
33	360	1,356	723	434	141
34	334	1,342	689	381	140
Total:	**25,519**	**82,804**	**52,573**	**18,545**	**3,045**

A majority of the respondents have a high school degree level of education. The next highest number of respondents have some college, followed by less than a high school degree, then a college degree, and then greater than a college degree. This is similar to the breakdown of education in the full sample, where a majority of the respondents have a highest educational attainment of a high school diploma. Similarly, the respondents in the restricted sample are clustered around the level of a high school diploma. This is interesting because it depicts a relationship much like the one I hypothesized in the previous part of this chapter; namely, that those with more education would be less likely to be living at home. Those with a college degree and those with more than a college degree have the least amount of people in their categories of those who are living at home.

4.8 Conclusions

The purpose of this section was to use the ACS to obtain descriptive statistics in an attempt to describe more recent trends of adults living at home. My intended outcome was to supplement the multivariate statistical analyses in the first portion of this chapter. While the timeliness of the data is a major strength of using these data, unfortunately I was not able to analyze the intricacies of various family development variables using these data. For instance, I was unable to estimate logistic regression equations predicting the log odds of being an adult living at home because the ACS did not provide me with data about adults not living at home, that is, the successfully launched adults. Beyond descriptive statistics, these data would not have been ideal to use in a major analysis for the purposes of my study.

Nevertheless, I feel that using the data to supplement my findings is quite important and enlightening. For example, the NSFH data did not permit me to analyze race/ethnic identification nor did they allow me to analyze Hispanic identification. I feel that including these variables is in fact quite important, as there is certainly a chance that the risk of living at home would vary by race/ethnicity and Hispanic identification.

By using the more current ACS data, I was able to look at the trend of adults living with their parents in a more contemporary light. The addition of these descriptive statistics tell us something about the contemporary situation of adult children living with their parents; they describe well this trend in terms of various demographic variables such as sex, race/ethnicity, Hispanic identification and educational attainment. The real strength of this chapter is the ability to see recent trends of a very important phenomenon. The next chapter of this book will detail the qualitative findings of my research on previously launched adults.

Chapter 5
Qualitative Results

Abstract This chapter describes the qualitative results which were gathered from approximately 50 in depth interviews with previously launched adults and their parents. I outline information regarding qualitative interview techniques and other aspects of qualitative research methodology. Five main themes were discovered through careful analysis of the qualitative interviews: (1) actualization and the after-effects of moving in with parents, (2) motivators and factors surrounding the move back home, (3) expectations and realities of reactions from peers and others about the move back home (4) respondents' social lives and how they are affected by moving back home, and (5) stigma management and rationalization techniques.

Keywords Qualitative • Stigma • Social Life • Peers • Interview

In my qualitative research I examined the experiences of college students and graduates who had either moved back home with their parents or never moved out of their parents home. I then conducted interviews with some of my original respondents' parents to see what factors could either contribute to or detract from a happy and functional parent and child co-residence. I will first discuss the results from my research with the previously launched adults themselves, and then I will turn to a discussion of the results from the interviews with the parents of the original respondents.

For the first portion of my qualitative analysis, I used data from 36 semi- structured in-depth qualitative interviews. The sample consisted of 20 men and 16 women and the age of the respondents ranged from 18 to 27 years at the time of the interviews. The names of the participants were replaced with pseudonyms to ensure anonymity. Other identifying characteristics, such as the respondents' university and hometown, were also changed.

I developed my sample of respondents using a purposive strategy as well as a snowball sampling approach. I interviewed participants in the locations of their choice. The interviews were conducted at their homes, restaurants, coffee shops, bookstores, and my office. Prior to conducting each interview, respondents were given a consent form they were asked to read and sign. I asked each respondent for demographic data, some of which were also gathered during the interview itself. Interviews lasted approximately 45 min–1 h and were tape recorded and subsequently transcribed.

© Springer International Publishing Switzerland 2016
D.N. Farris, *Boomerang Kids: The Demography of Previously Launched Adults*,
SpringerBriefs in Population Studies, DOI 10.1007/978-3-319-31227-9_5

The interview guide for my research consisted of open ended questions and was organized into three main themes: educational background of respondent and decisions for moving back home, effects of moving back in, and stigma related to moving back home. The interview questions mainly pertained to the respondents' experiences with and feelings about moving back home, as well as the reactions of friends, family, and new acquaintances. Additionally, I explored the dynamics of the familial relationship upon moving back home, and the likes and dislikes of being back at home. To conclude the interviews, I asked each respondent to give advice to someone who was going to be moving back home, based on the respondent's experiences of a similar situation.

I used a two-stage model of coding as described by Esterberg (2001). The initial stage, or open coding, was done to identify themes and categories that were of interest with regard to the research topic. By carefully re-reading the interview transcripts, I was able to see emerging and recurring themes. By using focused coding, I was able to look more closely at the themes and was able to group my data into important thematic categories. Using these techniques, I was able to identify several recurring patterns among college graduates who moved back in with their parents.

My research was informed by theories of the life course perspective, identity and self-esteem, and self-concept as these are related to a person being a member of a stigmatized group. All of the participants in my study reported individual circumstances that led them to move back home, as well as unique experiences while living at home. While each respondent's specific experience was ultimately different, many shared similarities. Five main themes emerged from the interviews: (1) actualization and the after-effects of moving in with parents, (2) motivators and factors surrounding the move back home, (3) expectations and realities of reactions from peers and others about the move back home (4) respondents' social lives and how they are affected by moving back home, and (5) stigma management and rationalization techniques.

The first theme pertained to the actualization and after-effects of moving home. For many respondents, having to move back in with their parents after graduation consisted of negative feelings about the event. Furman (2005) has suggested that making the decision to move back home with parents is a very difficult one for most "boomerangers." In my study, many respondents "weren't looking forward to it" and realized it was "a step backwards just going from freedom and kind of being out on your own to being back with your parents," but some did not seem to mind or think of it as a particularly major occurrence. One female respondent, Jean, decided to move in with her sister, brother in law, and their child, instead of moving back in with her parents, who lived close by. When asked how she felt about the move, she said:

It was not a good feeling, because I graduated early from high school very specifically to leave my small town and the thought of going to school for 4 years and work my butt off to get good grades, I really thought that I would have a better job lined up by the time I graduated so it was very disconcerting to have to go home and move back in with my parents after have living some- after having lived somewhere else for 4 years.

Some of the respondents did not have negative views on moving home. Lenny, a respondent who had returned home after studying abroad, felt that returning home would be "a homecoming in the sense that I wasn't burned out on my hometown." Two respondents, Loren and Allie, moved home with the expectation to student teach for a semester and then move out of the family home. They both stayed at home for longer than expected, but did not mind the move at first because it was supposed to be temporary. As Loren realized that was going to be living at home longer than expected, she reported being "happy, but not so excited. [It was] nice to be home because I missed them [parents] but I didn't want to be around them all the time." Another respondent, Layla, found a job in her hometown, which was the main reason she moved back in with parents. She moved home to take her job in as an financial planner, and "just, lived with my parents while I was studying to pass my licensing exams so I wouldn't have to work. I could actually study and make sure I passed them [exams]" and thought she would move out when she started her job. Bryan, an Ivy League graduate, was "not too worried about it" as friends were pressuring him to move to New York or Boston. With his financial situation out of control, Bryan said:

> I think it was more stressful thinking of moving to Boston of New York without having money so it was more of like I felt safe moving back home. Just because you know, my parents won't expect too much as long as I take care of myself, keep after myself, then they don't really worry about me so...

Louise and Clayton were among the respondents who had the most negative expectations regarding the move back home. When asked how he felt about moving back home, Clayton replied, "It sucks." Louise was worried about a main obstacle to moving back home: privacy—or lack thereof. Furman (2005) noted that while adults may be gaining many things by moving back home, "you'd also be giving up a lot, including your privacy, a certain amount of autonomy, and the ability to choose your own brand of toilet paper" (2005: 24). When asked about how she felt when she realized she was going to be moving back home, Louise said:

> I was definitely nervous. Lack of privacy, moving back in, if we would have conflicts and arguments like when I was in high school and also my cat. I brought my cat and my mom didn't want me to bring the cat at first...I was a little bit worried just mainly about the privacy and I guess my own personal freedom even though, like I had it for 4 and ½ years, and losing that when I came back, and I lost a little bit but it wasn't as bad as I thought.

While the responses from the participants about their feelings of moving back home varied, during the duration of the interview all respondents expressed some discontent with living back at home. Respondents were hesitant and dismayed at the prospect of moving home because of what it meant in terms of their identity. They saw themselves as going from being independent, self-sufficient, successful young adults to living back at home with parents. Those who were college graduates had identities that were strongly correlated with their roles as students, and now they had reached a point in their lives where they had no clear-cut defined role expectations. They were in a transitional and unfamiliar territory, and moving back

home with parents forced them to renegotiate their self-concepts as a result of now
belonging to a different social group.

The second main theme pertained to the motivations surrounding the move
home. I believe this to be the most important theme from my qualitative research on
previously launched adults. There were multiple reasons why respondents moved
back home with parents, but three main motivations emerged. One motivation was
lack of employment following graduation from college. Another motivation for
moving home was the chance to "regroup" due to a lack of other alternatives. The
third motivation, financial stress, was the most common among respondents and
seemed to be an underlying motivation for most of the respondents to move back
home or stay at home. While some respondents made no mention of money as a
determining factor of why they chose to move back or stay at home so long, each of
the respondents reported that the free rent, free food, and no bills were among the
main reasons they enjoyed living back at home.

Among many of the respondents who moved home and subsequently moved out
on their own, finances were one of the reasons they cited as to why they stayed so
long. One respondent, Loren, said that she was not sure of how long she wanted to
stay at home. "It was debatable, I wanted to wait until I started making some money
first, my main goal was to make some money," and that is why she lived at home for
a year before moving out on her own. Interestingly, a different respondent's main
reason for staying home was finances, but not lack of. Robby said:

> I could live on my own and support myself, save money but I'm in a situation right now
> where 90%, 90 to 95% of my paycheck is going straight to my bank account...I mean, I'm
> 24 years old, I been out of school 2 years and I mean I've got more money in my bank
> account than I can, I guarantee any 24 year old does. I mean, if I live at home another year,
> I'm going to have you know over $100,000 in the bank. Talk about cash, no debt, so, I mean
> I've already started a Roth IRA for my retirement, tax free retirement, put the max amount
> in this year, put the max amount next year, and put the max amount in until I retire, so hope-
> fully I'll have a couple million by the time I want to retire. Tax free, so. Maybe live at home
> a couple years early, it's a lot easier later on in life. So... we'll see how that one goes
> though.

This respondent's experience was most certainly atypical when talking about money
and financial situations, although his story could be used to describe some of the
perks of living at home. Once at home, the decisions to stay or move out were also
varied from respondent to respondent. Financial reasons were an underlying factor
for many of the respondents who chose to move back home. Experts are calling this
generation "Generation D" (for debt) and "Generation B" (for bankrupt) (Furman
2005). For example, one male respondent, Clayton, was in debt and had no other
option to move home. He said:

> I'm paying all school for myself you know, so I've got $57,000 worth of loans right now.
> And I need a new car so... it makes sense not to pay for rent or money... you know in terms
> of money like I need to pay, start paying off those loans as much as I can as soon as I can,
> I'm already going to be paying for them for years and years.

Clayton was only one of my respondents who was deep into financial debt and
really had no other option but to move home and pay down his student loans. Other

respondents cited financial reasons for their decisions to move home, but more in the sense of saving money, not paying down a large sum of accruing loans. Three other respondents also decided to move home because of financial reasons. One female respondent, Maria, has a daughter, and was also in debt from school, and not knowing exactly what she wanted to do and a lack of financial independence limited her options of what she was going to be able to do after she graduated. She had some idea, but said that:

> It's rough to have a little girl, and, I'm in debt (laughing). So I didn't really want to just jump into a job because I knew that I was going to have to leave it sooner or later to go to school.

Bryan, a male respondent, decided to move back home after living in the Northeast and attending an Ivy League University. His parents were unable to help him pay for his schooling, but he was able to get half of his education paid for. This left him with about $87,000 in school loans. As I have previously stated, the thought of moving to another Northeastern city left Bryan feeling stressed out and upset, and when asked about his situation he said the following:

> Really the only reason at first was finances. Most of my friends were moving to like Boston and New York, which are insanely expensive, and I didn't even have enough money to like relocate if I wanted to. So I was like I'll just move back home, maybe save some money and then move out there...So at first it was strictly financial but now its more of like I'm sort of here to help my little brother too 'cause my parents' relationship is really rocky and I don't know I just feel like he needs another male person in the house to like make sure he goes to college and everything. So and those are really the only two reasons but other than that. So like mainly finances, I mean I'm trying to save money to like buy a car.

Bryan went on to say that while he first thought his move was going to be only temporary, he is thinking of waiting until his younger brother graduates from high school, which will be in 4 years. Another respondent, Lenny, was living abroad for 9 months, and described that "when I moved back from Spain I didn't have any money and so I decided to move home... I didn't have a better plan. I didn't have any money so..."

As I have previously stated, respondents moved home for a variety of reasons and continued to live at home for a number of other reasons. These reasons coincide with those put forth by Furman (2005), which include financial problems such as high credit card or student loan debt, tight job markets and the lack of employment opportunities, the prohibitive cost of housing, and in some cases, a reluctance to grow up and accept responsibilities. For many of the respondents, a lack of alternatives was another factor in their decision to move home. Today, more resources and skill accumulation are required before a successful launching to adulthood can be completed. While rational choice theory may be an over-simplistic notion of human nature, it is certainly applicable to my respondents and their decisions to move back home. Some may believe that in deciding to move back home after graduating from college, an individual will incur more costs than benefits. However it is clear that moving home provides a stable situation where the individuals have a lower likelihood of failure as opposed to moving out and venturing the world on one's own.

The third theme pertained to the reactions of my respondents' friends and peers. One of my research questions pertained to the self-esteem, self-appraisal, and identity of those who returned home. I hypothesized that returning home would have a detrimental effect on the "boomeranger's" self-esteem, and that the individual's peers would have negative and/or judgmental reactions. As I have previously stated, symbolic interactionism was the primary theoretical paradigm utilized in this study, and the writings of

Mead and Cooley provided the framework around which my research project was centered. Symbolic interactionism is the idea that meanings are given to situations through interaction and interpretation. If our self evaluations are affected by the evaluations that others have of us and how we perceive those evaluations (Mead 1934) and utilize the reactions of others to provide the viewpoint from which we come to define our attributes (Cooley 1902), then negative reactions from others would in turn make our perception of ourselves to be less favorable and thus have an adverse effect on our self-esteem.

Contrary to my expectations, respondents reported that they did not experience any negative reactions from their peers or friends. Despite this, as I will discuss later, many of the respondents utilized stigma management, rationalizations and justifications when talking to me about their experiences. This led me to believe that despite the fact that they did not receive overtly negative reactions from friends and peers, the respondents still felt that they were engaging in a behavior that was unusual or abnormal. When asked whether friends and peers had negative reactions about respondents moving home, most of the respondents reported that their friends and peers did not. Many of the respondents said that their friends were understanding of their particular situations, and thought it was the best decision for each respondent. Additionally, some of the respondents had close friends or significant others who had also returned home, and some even reported friends who were jealous of the fact that they were living at home again.

One respondent, Layla, explained that her friends and co-workers' response was:

> Actually they were like "oh that's so smart, you're saving a lot of money"… Like "your parents live in town, you get along with them, like y'all have a good relationship anyways. I wish I would have lived with my parents for a while, I wish I would have been able to save up money" and stuff like that. And also I think because I was so young, like everyone I work with is a lot older than me.

As far as friends being jealous, one respondent described his co-workers as "being all jealous." Likewise, Elise, a female respondent, said her friends told her that she should "move home you know if you don't have a job… just stay away from the job market, and they all thought it was a positive thing I guess." She said that she was happy that her friends did not make her feel bad about moving home, and after she moved home she traveled to Africa to work with children in Rwanda. She finished her travels in Africa, and is living at home again until she finds a job.

Three of the female respondents all had significant others who had also returned to the home of their parents. Ruthie said that her boyfriend "understood because he went back home too after he graduated in May, he went back home for the summer and we were both kind of at home and complaining about our parents together." When asked how her romantic interest reacted to her decision to move back home, Allie said that "the romantic interest, he was actually living at home too, so he couldn't really say anything." Layla said her coworkers did not have negative reactions to her move, and neither did her friends. She said:

> Well two of my friends that lived in my hometown lived with their parents too so... obviously they didn't care. None of my friends cared, none of my friends were like "Oh you're a loser" ...I don't think anybody really cared. And, I guess I was like semi dating with someone but he lived with his parents too.

Two respondents, Jean and Shane said that they discussed the move with their significant others, who at the time were living in different cities than they were. Jean said that she and her boyfriend had discussed her situation and "decided that maybe, that maybe it was the best decision for my life at that point." Shane, who plans on moving to be with his girlfriend in the future, said that his friends' reactions were "no one way or the other. They didn't really say" and his girlfriend "knew it was best for the time being. And that eventually we would get together." For Jean and Shane, moving home was a decision that would affect not only their own lives, but the lives of their long-term partners as well. They discussed the decision with their partners, and as a dyad decided that it would be the best thing to do at the time in order to save money and get their lives more on track.

While most of the respondents' friends, peers and significant others had favorable reactions to the respondents moving back home, two respondents' friends had ambivalent reactions to them moving back home. Allie expressed that one of her friends in particular said "just that my town is lame, don't go back. And to go somewhere else. Mainly my friend was asking me to move to Houston." When asked how she felt about her friend's reaction, Allie said, "I kind of felt the same way. I didn't really want to come back home but it made the most sense so..." When asked about his friends' reactions, Clayton said "two of my friends kind of wanted me to live with them at first but they you know, they did the same thing as me [moved home after graduation]." Jean had an experience with the locals in her town when she returned home and was working at a restaurant there to help pay bills while living at her sister's house. When I asked her if she had met anyone new living back at home, and if they had any reactions to her moving back, she said:

> I mean I was working at a restaurant that I hadn't worked at before but my sister had worked at, so I mean I knew some of the people but a lot of the people were new so I mean I had to explain to them that I was living at home.
> I: And did they have any specific reactions?
> I mean some people would like make jokes about it like "Oh well you went to school and you just had to come home and move home with your parents" so I mean it wasn't really that big of a deal because they were all waiters in my town so I mean. [I: So they didn't make you feel...] Right, yeah. There's no one in my town that was gonna make me feel insecure about graduating from college and coming and living at home. You know what I mean?

Despite the co-workers' reactions and jokes, Jean took the incident at work in stride and remained confident in her abilities as an independent young woman. She went on to explain to me that moving home with the intentions of looking for jobs elsewhere did not work out as she had expected, as she felt obligated to help her sister and parents with things. Because of this, she moved back to her college town to live with her boyfriend and take a job as a manager at a restaurant where she had been previously employed during college.

Finding out that friends and peers had generally indifferent reactions to the respondents moving home was surprising. There are likely a variety of reasons for the reactions that respondents described. There is a likelihood that the friends and peers really did not care about the respondents returning home, or it could possibly be the case that the friends and peers were worried about being in the same situation of having to move back in with their own parents.

The fourth theme, the respondents' social lives, was disclosed in a variety of the interviews I conducted. Information about the respondents' social lives was revealed by questions such as "How did you feel about moving back home?" "Do you have any privacy issues?" and "What do you dislike the most about living back at home?" I found that the respondents' social lives were altered or hampered in some way as a direct result of living back at home. Many of my respondents discussed a change in social life and behaviors after being asked how they felt when they realized they were going to be returning home. They described the reality of the situation of living at home and how they changed some behaviors out of respect for their parents while living back at home. Similarly, the respondents noted the difficulty associated with meeting potential mates while living back at home. Respondents noted that meeting someone and bringing him/her back to the family home for sexual relations would not only be disrespectful, but also had the potential to be awkward. The awkwardness associated with negotiating sexual relationships was apparent regardless of whether the respondent was in a serious relationship or was looking to engage in a more casual sexual encounter.

When I asked Robby if he had met any women while he was living at home, he responded:

> Yeah that's a good question. Living at home with your parents does hamper your social life, that's for sure. Not in the aspect that you can't bring them [women] home or, anything like that but just you don't hang out with your friends as much, I don't think. Which in turn you don't meet as many people, no, social life definitely slowed down when I moved home. Now that I moved home.

Other respondents described similar experiences. Joffrey and Bryan both said that they thought part of the reason they had not gotten into relationships with people was because they were still living at home. Joffrey said:

> Yeah well I don't think it's because I live at home but I definitely have been single since I've been there. And it might, I don't know at one side it's I don't feel like I should be bringing a girl back to their house, since it is their house and not mine. But I don't know I've also been pretty busy so that's another reason why I haven't...

Bryan said that he thinks that if he met someone and had to tell them he was living at home "it would be difficult to do," and he has not been trying to find someone to date since "living at home." Not only did respondents describe not being able to start relationships because of living at home, they also discussed the awkwardness associated with bringing a member of the opposite sex home, whether they were dating this person or just "hooking up." Respondents Robby, Clayton, and Alex discussed the difficulty of negotiating a sexual relationship with a partner while living back at home. When asked about whether he experienced any privacy issues living back at home, Robby said:

> Oh there's definitely a privacy issue because my parents' room is directly across from my room and they sleep with the door open so the room looks straight at my room, so if I want to bring a girl home it makes it a little bit difficult with, for them not to know. I mean I could do it, they wouldn't care, but it's kind of like I don't want my parents knowing about that so.

Shane, who was in a long term, long distance relationship, indicated annoyance with his situation when his girlfriend would visit from out of town. Shane said that his sister would "barge in on me and my girlfriend when I really don't want her to be in here [his room]." He said that she would not knock on the door, and his girlfriend thought it was "odd and weird." Situations where there is a lack of privacy could potentially place a strain on long term, long distance relationships where the partners were only able to see each other sporadically. Shane said that the lack of privacy when his girlfriend was visiting was the one thing he hated the most about living at home.

I asked respondents to discuss what it was like when they were trying to meet potential partners. Clayton said "people don't want to come back to your house if your parents are going to be in the living room, you know?" Similarly, Alex said that he "hasn't brought any girls over, because that's kind of awkward."

Some said that while they still felt comfortable going outside of the parents' home and meeting to party with friends, they did not feel as comfortable bringing friends over to the house. Loren, Alex and Lenny expressed these feelings when asked about their likes and dislikes of living at home. Loren said that she "still felt bad having a lot of friends over, just 'cause it's an intrusion on them [parents]. So, having lots of friends over and that would probably be the only thing that really wasn't, that I didn't like." Alex said that he "doesn't like to bring people over to the house to party and stuff like that." I asked respondents what their least favorite aspect of living at home was, and Lenny replied:

> I like to be very social. I like to have di-, like not parties, but I'd say dinner parties and I don't have not even the facilities to myself at all times and I don't have, I don't have exclusive privilege over the domain of my house.

Lenny described to me feelings of having to be considerate of others living in the house, and thought that having dinner parties would not only be a strain on his parents, but he felt that since the house was not his, he did not have the right to ask everyone to leave so he could host something.

In conjunction with privacy issues, some respondents described instances in which their parents treated them like young children again. When Lee was living at home, his mother would wake him up in the mornings, "which was weird," and Clayton described his mother waking him up as well. With more of a favorable reaction toward the experience, he said, "Mom makes sure I wake up in the morning 'cause I'm a heavy sleeper, you know, and then come home and eat dinner around the table, you know?" Layla described disliking her experiences of her parents asking where she was going and with whom:

> *I guess the biggest adjustment, was that you get so used to not having to tell anybody where you are, no one's really being concerned with where you are, and when I would leave to go out, my parents would be like "Where are y'all going?" It's like "What do you mean where am I going, I'm going to a bar" you know what I mean? I guess I could tell them but I was always just like "We don't really know where we're going" because it's, that was one of the only awkward things. When I was getting ready to go out and my parents would still be sitting down on the couch watching TV and I would go to leave and I would be like "Okay I'm leaving" and my parents were like "Bye!!" and everything, it's just like, I'm 23 years old, why am I saying bye to my parents before I go out? That was awkward, that was the only thing that was awkward I guess.*

Ruthie said that while it was nice to be able to regroup and have someone take care of her, she kept "asking them [her parents] to treat me more like a person and less like a small child." Ruthie said that her mother would follow her around and give her very little privacy, and said that "she'd [her mother] follow me to the bathroom talking to me and I'm like "MOM! Can you please leave, I have to pee!"…it was bad." To a lesser extreme, Elise had to alter her life somewhat after moving back home. In regards to privacy issues, she said, "To a certain extent there are. When I'm on the phone with my friends I don't want to be like "Hey I met this really cute guy" in front of my parents or anything." She also said, "They don't really expect [me to do] a lot. They don't expect more than they expected in high school, they expect less probably."

For an adult child, moving back home can be an extremely life changing experience. The change from living completely on one's own to living with parents again can be challenging to one's social life. Bringing members of the opposite sex home, starting relationships, and maintaining independence proved to be rather challenging for some previously launched adults. However, trading bills and responsibilities for a few minor social setbacks seemed like a good situation for some, and my respondents tried to make the best out of their situations. Social interaction is paramount for maintaining relationships. Moving back home not only caused one's social network to change, but also to shrink in a sense. Students in college have vast amounts of peers, professors, and friends with whom to interact and build interpersonal relationships. Moving back home can decrease the size of a social network to include only family members and close friends. Comparing the present social life of someone to one's past social life or even the social lives of others can have an effect on one's satisfaction (Buunk et al. 2007). If one's needs are not met as a result of a diminished social life, as is apparent in the lives of many of the respondents in the study, happiness and satisfaction could suffer.

The last theme I found in my qualitative research was that of stigma management and rationalizations surrounding living back at home with parents. While the data suggested that respondents' self-esteem and identities were not adversely affected by their moving back home, each of them offered what Goffman (1963) referred to as stigma management techniques. Stigma refers to a characteristic that is unusual and detrimental with regard to the moral status of the signifier. The term, according to Goffman, refers to an attribute that is deeply discrediting. I was concerned with stigma with regard to one's character, and found that many respondents indirectly justified their living back at home. Respondents also offered rationalizations for the behavior. Matza and Sykes (1957) described techniques of neutralization that individuals often use to justify actions in terms of rationalizations. Rationalizations are developed subsequent to deviant behavior (in this case, moving back home with parents), and are offered to "protect the individual from self-blame and the blame of others after the act" (1957:666). Respondents used their age and status as a college graduate as a main rationalization for living back at home. The recentness of graduating, being the youngest person at the workplace, and trying to attain goals (such as getting into graduate school or obtaining an internship) were some of the rationalizations that respondents offered to me during the interviews.

Layla said that she did not feel uncomfortable about living back at home because "it wasn't like I was 30 years old and living in my parent's basement." Likewise, Ruthie said that she knows living back at home "is only temporary, it's not like I plan on living with my mom for the next 10 years, but I would never move home and not really do anything." Those who were college graduates used this status to justify why they were living at home. Lee said that graduating from college and then moving back home "wasn't like dropping out and having to move back home." Loren and Lenny also felt the same way. I asked respondents if they thought moving back home was socially acceptable, and Loren replied:

> I don't think it's acceptable if you're not going to do anything and you're just taking advantage of it. But, I definitely think it's different with a college degree because obviously I want to do something with my life it's not just like I'm just being there to be lazy.

Lenny "tries to raise the understanding with people that I meet that I'm not just a bum sleeping on my parents couch." He also said that having a college degree makes one a valued member of society. He feels his situation is also different because he has a full time "real" job. Layla also used the "real job" justification as to why it was more socially acceptable for her to be living back at home. Layla said, "If I wouldn't have had a job already and had go home and live with my parents, I would have felt like a failure."

Some respondents joked about their situations as ways to minimize the severity of the situation. Loren and Clayton both used jokes when asked about how they felt when they told someone new that they were living back at home. Clayton said "I usually tell them [people I meet] it's roommates, that I live with roommates. Roommates I've known since I was born." Likewise, Loren said that she "likes to call them her roommates." Elise also said that she has to joke about her situation and "be lighthearted, in a way, because I do feel a little bit like a loser." Joking was respondents' way of "exercising something other than tact" (Goffman 1963: 136) and taking the main focus off their stigmatizing attribute in uncomfortable situations.

Another justification respondents used was blaming others, or denying responsibility. Denial of responsibility is one of the five ways rationalization occurs (Matza and Sykes 1957). For example, when I asked Layla why she had lived with her parents for such a long period of time, she said:

> That wasn't really my choice. I wanted to move out once I started working or at least a month after I started working because I had the money to do it. I had a good enough job to live on my own and I wanted to live on my own with my friends. But then they didn't end up getting jobs so they didn't have the means to move out on their own, so then I was basically living with my parents waiting for them to find jobs, waiting for them to decide to move out, and I got tired of waiting.

Like Layla, Robby said that he could afford to move out on his own if he wanted to. However, Robby was the only respondent who kept justifying his decision to stay home in terms of the extreme monetary rewards he was gaining from living at home. He discussed his financial situation many times during our interview. Exchange theory (Blau 1964) states that we analyze our decisions in terms of the relative costs and rewards we will incur as a result of said decisions. Like many respondents, saving money was one of the things Robby liked most about living at home, and apparently the amount he was saving was one of the biggest reasons for him to continue living at home for 2 years. During the interviews, I asked respondents why they decided to move back home, but I never made it seem as if they needed to offer justifications for doing so. Nevertheless, many of the respondents offered different rationalizations on their own, whether or not they were aware of doing so.

I explored the experiences of young adults, mainly college graduates who moved back home with their parents and college students who lived with their parents. Respondents faced living at home with negative emotions, but many conveyed that the end result was not as bad as they had predicted it would be. Respondents lived at home for various reasons, but finances were a main motivator for a majority of respondents. Respondents did not appear to outwardly suffer from any damage to their self-esteem or self-appraisal as a result of moving back home. Friends and peers of the respondents did not have negative or judgmental reactions to the respondents moving back home. However, my respondents used rationalizations and justifications for their decisions during the interviews. Previous research (Clemens and Axelson 1985; Goldscheider and Goldscheider 1989, 1998; Schnaiberg and Goldenberg 1989; Mitchell and Gee 1996; Mitchell 1998) has focused mainly on how parents felt and were affected by adult children returning home. Literature on self-esteem and identity can be related to my study, but the findings of various studies of marginalized groups did not correspond with my findings of this particular group. Those that go against group norms, such as moving back home when expected to move out and on with one's life, may well face prejudice or discrimination from those who do not go against the norms (Rubin and Hewstone 1998; Hogg and Reid 2006). Next, I turn to a discussion of the qualitative research that I conducted with the parents of some of my original respondent pool.

For this portion of the project, I interviewed some of the parents of my previous respondents, and inquired about the division of household labor that the parents experienced while their adult child was living at home. For my first qualitative analysis, I asked respondents about various aspects of household chores and tasks, and I compared their answers to those of their parents. I also asked the parents about satisfaction derived from their children living back at home, and I inquired about general good and bad aspects of the child returning home in the opinions of both the parent and the child.

Division of labor in the household is an important aspect of satisfaction with family life. Coltrane notes that the five most "time consuming major household tasks (in the United States) include (a) meal preparation or cooking, (b) housecleaning, (c) shopping for groceries and household goods, (d) washing dishes or cleaning up after meals, and (e) laundry, including washing, ironing, and mending clothes." (2000: 1210). While many modern heterosexual couples espouse egalitarian ideology, and there has been an increase in fathers' involvement with childrearing and housework, women still do two to three times more of the housework (Coltrane 2000; Milkie et al. 2002). While husbands may happily share in portions of the housework, women feel more responsible for the home and children (Hochschild and Machung 1989). This housework can include various aspects of child-rearing, such as cooking, laundry, feeding and cleaning (2002).

While the focus of my particular study is on adult children returning to the home, rather than younger children living at home, many of these components may likely be operating in a household where an adult child is living. Coltrane argues that "housework is embedded in complex and shifting patterns of social relations" and that "housework cannot be understood without realizing how it is related to gender, household structure, family interaction, and the operation of both formal and informal market economies" (2000: 1209). The complexity of housework and the negotiation of household tasks can be seen in light of adult children moving back home. Adult children who have once lived on their own may be used to taking care of themselves, but there is a chance that they will revert back to behavior they once engaged in while formerly living with their parents, often a time when they were much younger. An interesting distinction would be to look at the differences in the experiences between mothers and fathers who have children returning home. The return of an adult child may have more detrimental effects on the mother's happiness, as women may be generally expected to run the household, and the return of an adult child may impose more demands on the mother than on the father. There may be more of an imposition on mothers of adult children who move back home as far as time and housework demands are concerned, but mothers may judge the unequal distribution of labor as fair or expected (Coltrane 2000). Additionally, mothers who engage in employment outside the home may experience more stress due to the balance of work and family demands (Hochschild and Machung 1989; Mitchell 1998).

For the second part of this project, I interviewed four of the original respondents' parents. These parents had occupations such as insurance agent, teacher, CFO, and human resources manager at a car dealership. Two of the parents interviewed were still married (to each other), one was divorced and one was divorced and remarried. Three of the respondents were women and one was a man.

The names of the participants were replaced with pseudonyms to ensure anonymity. As with the original portion of this project, the sample was gathered using a purposive strategy as well as snowball sampling. I interviewed participants in locations of their choice. The interviews were conducted at their homes, restaurants, coffee shops, bookstores, and my office. Prior to conducting each interview, respondents were given a consent form that they were asked to read and sign. I asked each respondent for demographic data, some of which was also gathered during the interview itself. Interviews lasted approximately 45 min to one and one half hour and were tape recorded and subsequently transcribed.

For this project, the interview questions primarily pertained to how the parents felt about their adult child moving back home, how the move back home affected the housework and other aspects of the household, and what the parents liked and disliked about having their adult child living back at home. This project was not intended to generalize to all parents of adult children who move back home. Rather, the purpose is to describe the experiences and feelings of the parents that were interviewed for this particular study. The findings are meant to serve as a starting point for further research on the topic of previously launched adults, as these experiences relate to the adult children and their parents.

5.1 Findings

Many of my findings coincide with the previous research done on adult children living back at home. Surprisingly, the parents in my study did not report an adverse affect on household labor when their adult children moved back home. In fact, many of the adult children were quite self sufficient when it came to doing household tasks that may have added to the workload of their parents with the return home. One respondent, Robby (27 years old, at home for 2 years), described the following of his chore situation:

Cleaning ladies come and clean the house, and make my bed once a week and I do my own laundry... I'm kind of a stickler, I like my laundry done the right way so...I do my own laundry but I would assume she would probably do it if I didn't do it but I do my own laundry and, I don't really have to do dishes or anything which is nice.

Robby's living situation was atypical of the rest of my respondent pool. Robert's father is an engineer and his mother is a hospital administrator. Like many of the upper class families discussed in Hondagneu-Sotelo's work (2007), Robby's family has the privilege of employing a domestic worker to take care of the household tasks, so it may be the case that even if Robby's move back home had added more work to the household, it would not be the responsibility of his parents to take up this extra work.

Another respondent, Shane (24 years old, at home for one and a half years), discussed the negotiation of living back at home with his mother and sister. Shane explained that in his situation, "[my mother] charged rent...we came to the decision and decided when I was going to get a job and when I did get a job I would start paying rent to my mom to help her out a little bit because she paid for a lot of my school loans and stuff, so..." Interestingly, during our interview, Shane neglected to inform me of how much he was actually paying to his mother per month to be living back in her home. When I interviewed his mother, Margaret (divorced, human resources manager), she told me "I felt like it was the only right thing to do [let him move back home]. He did pay me $200.00 a month for rent and groceries... it was too expensive to keep him in an apartment until he found a job." Not only did Margaret feel like it was her responsibility to house Shane when he had been unable to find a job, it seems as though she felt like it would be her responsibility to finance the cost required for him to live away from her, in his own separate apartment. Like many of my respondents, Shane enjoyed the comfort of living at home with his mother while not having to worry about "much responsibility" and "not have to worry about upkeep on the house or yard." Margaret noted that having Shane back "did not affect my household too much... I guess I cooked more often and that would be about all... he pretty much took care of himself."

Another respondent, Mary (married, high school teacher), revealed that the amount of housework she spent time on when her daughter Layla moved home stayed the same. When asked about the effect of her child moving back home on the amount of housework, Mary responded, "It stayed the same. She functioned upstairs in her own space which didn't affect us until she moved out and we had to disinfect her space again." Similar to previous research on previously launched adults, Mary and her husband David (CFO) said that they did not have a problem with Layla moving back home, because she had found a job and was living at home with the intention of working and supporting herself to move out. David said, "She needed a place to live until she passed her certification test to work at an insurance company in our hometown. She asked us if it was okay, and we thought it was not a problem, we knew and understood the reason. We knew it would be short term."

Another respondent, Jeanne (divorced/remarried, insurance agent), whose 22 year old daughter moved back in with her after living on her own for about a year and a half, had a similar response to Mary. Jeanne noted, "My housework stayed the same. My daughter was expected to keep common areas tidy and neat, like clean up after herself. I ask her to clean her dishes and put them in the dishwasher and do her own laundry. I do expect that if I ask for help with something that she is agreeable."

While the parents interviewed denied any change in amount of housework, I think it is important to note that there were clear disparities between what the parents reported had changed, and what a researcher could see had changed. For example, Margaret telling me that Shane took care of himself, but the fact that she "cooked more" clearly indicates that having him back at home led to more housework, such as cooking and cleaning up after meal preparation. Adding another person to the weekly menu probably added cost to the grocery bills, and while Shane did pay some money to Margaret for "groceries and rent," it is impossible to determine whether or not it was adequately covering the extra expenses Margaret incurred with Shane living back in her home. Margaret also disclosed that Shane was expected "to keep up with his room and wash his own clothes," but failed to mention anything about keeping common areas clean and tidy, like the living room or kitchen. It seems as though the parents may be under the impression that their amount of work stayed the same with an adult child living back at home, a closer examination of the interview transcripts and the respondents' answers reveal that this is not the case.

Another disparity can be found in the responses of Mary and Layla. When asked about the expectations she had for Layla to contribute around the house, Mary told me that "she was asked to clean up after herself…although her room and bathroom were a wreck when she moved out anyway." Like Mary had stated earlier in the interview, she knew that when Layla moved out she would have to "disinfect her space" again. This seemingly full scale cleaning procedure could most certainly be seen as adding the extra burden of housework that comes with having an adult child living back at home, although Mary did not make it seem like having Layla living back at home, or subsequently moving out of the family home, was that big of an issue.

Something that emerged from my data that I did not previously anticipate were the respondents' discussion of the changes in the psycho-social demands of having an adult child living back at home. Like Hochschild discusses, wives feel more responsible for the homes and the children (1989: 463). Having adult children moving back home brings with it the issue of again worrying about the children. When children are away at college, parents seem to get by with a somewhat "out of sight, out of mind" mentality. My interviews revealed that mothers who had children return home worried about the whereabouts of their children again. For example, Mary described a rule that she had for her daughter Layla, "She had a curfew… but there was the 'worry factor.' When kids are living away, you are on a 'need to know' basis. When kids are at home, that goes away. I worried about where she was and what she was doing." Likewise, Jeanne said that "there were rules put in place that she [my daughter] is to communicate to me her whereabouts. For example, if you go out with a friend, you tell me what time you are coming back. If that time were to change, you are expected to call with an update." When asked what she disliked the least about having her child back at home, Jeanne said "There is worry when she is out at night. If I wake up [while she's gone] I worry that she is okay. There is also stress when she is ill, and I guess to tell you the truth I'm sort of concerned on whether she will live with me forever."

Consequently, parents' worry was one of the exact things that the children disliked about moving back home. Layla said that she disliked

> having to tell someone where I'm going, like I know that's considerate and everything you know you get so used to… You know like I would go downstairs during the summer and I would be leaving to go study and my mom would be like 'where are you off to, and where are you going' and it's like a little stupid thing but when you're used to doing what you want when you want to do it, it can be annoying to have to check in with your parents all the time.

Similarly, the issue of privacy is something that the respondents discussed as one of the negatives of living back home. Robby said that "Not as much privacy, I mean, I mean it has its pros and cons you know I'd say your social life is hampered a little bit…" Shane also noted that his least favorite part about living back home was "The lack of privacy. And that's pretty much it, yeah. That's the only thing I hate about being here."

It seems that where parents have the most concern is the same place that children have the most annoyance. In some ways, it would make sense to think that a parent would not worry for a child once again living under their roof, especially one who is an adult, self sufficient, taking care of themselves, and not adding to the work or stress load. However, this is certainly not the case. It seems that mothers never stop mothering, despite the age of their children. Not only did mothers experience different psycho-social aspects related to their adult children being home, adult children being home altered family dynamics (sometimes in negative ways) as well. Jeanne disclosed to me that:

> I think that there was more of an effect on her [my daughter's] step-father as their relationship was never really that close and there was always tension between the two. In that respect the change in the household was that I was once again in a position of balancing the situation and keeping everything and every calm and smooth... she thinks that he picks on her and he thinks that she is rude and disrespectful... so that's hard.

As described in previous research (Aquilino and Supple 1991), tension and conflict can arise when an adult child moves home, particularly to the home of a blended family or one with stepparents. This tension can obviously be exacerbated if the adult child and their parent or stepparent do not get along well. Despite these tensions, it appears that Jeanne is generally happy with her daughter living back at home. Jeanne told me that Molly "helps with her stepfather's business...like filing and faxing and stuff like that. She also helps sometimes in the garden with watering and planting and she does sometimes mop the floors.... Although I guess that may be because her dog pees on them."

While the social lives' of the adult children is a topic that has been fully explored in the first portion of study, it would have been interesting to ask the parents' about their social lives as well. This obviously does not relate to the division of labor within the household, but it could certainly yield some interesting results for a study of a different kind. Some parents note having their "own lives" once their children move out and may experiences feelings of resent or uncertainty when their child moves back home and disrupts their pattern.

While my data reveal that there were certainly some negative aspects related to adult children moving back home, both the children and the parents reported overall positive experiences. Mary told me that she "liked getting to know her [daughter] at a different level; conversations take on a different perspective. There's a lot of change between high school and college, but you hope that some of the values you tried to instill remain." Shane's mother, Margaret, revealed that she "misses Shane now that he's moved out. I liked having him back home for the company and our talks about life, politics... anything. I miss that now." Jeanne told me that she liked having her daughter back home because "she can be company for errands... and she can be entertaining at times. She's also a good opponent for playing Wii." While parents reported happiness with having their children back home for the company or companionship, it seems that the adult children reported liking living back at home for the reason that they were basically able to be treated like a child in some ways again. Free or minimal rent, bills, and other expenses were the main motivations for the adult children report happiness living at home or for staying at home longer than they expected. However, adult children also discussed liking the company and companionship that living back at home provided. Shane told me that, "my mom and my sister, they're pretty much like my friends…I mean I bullshit around a lot with my mom… so it's pretty fun being back I guess."

Albeit in different ways, children and parents both seemed to experience positive aspects of adult children living at back at home and the negative experiences or increases in amount of work done by parents was negligible, at least in the reports of the parents I interviewed. For the most part, the parents in this study did not report having an increase in housework or other household divisions of labor when their adult children moved back home. However, there could be an issue of social desirability in that the parents did not want to disclose information that may lead them, or their children, to be seen in a negative light. Additionally, as I have previously stated, parents (mothers especially) may have been in fact doing more work around the house and either not realizing it, or naturalizing it as part of their job as a mother. The idea that the parents did not report to me that anything had changed as far as their household labor was concerned could be related to the idea of "total motherhood" in which mothers are expected to "optimize every dimension of children's lives" (Wolf 2007). Perhaps the mothers in my study neglected to think of having their children home as extra work, as they were just doing their "job" to help their children get back on their feet and into a stable environment. Another aspect of the disparity between the respondents in my two samples could be that the adult children over report their participation in household labor.

One implication of my research relates to the factors surrounding respondents' decisions to move back home or live at home. This study showed that finances were the main reason many of the respondents moved home. A prevalent theme in the economic climate of today is the idea that our generation is the first one that will not be able to attain an equal or better level of living than our parents, and this is certainly a disconcerting thought for many young people. A college degree is no longer a guarantee of a good job and comfortable life. However, it is reassuring to see that while there are changes in the economy, there are also changes in parent/child relationships as well as views on the life course. Changes in the life course are directly related to the economic situation of our times. Life course trajectory assumes that young adults are expected to transition to adulthood on a linear path of well-timed events, such as employment, marriage, and parenting (Elder 1998). However, several aspects of this trajectory vary among the youth population of today. Children are graduating from college, getting jobs or continuing schooling, but moving back home and delaying marriage and families. Parents are becoming more accommodating of this behavior, and children returning home may not be as big of an issue as it once was.

My qualitative research was not intended to be generalized to all young adults who live with or who have moved back in with their parents and the parents of these adult children. Rather, its purpose was to describe the experiences and feelings of those young adults and parents who were interviewed. Lack of generalizability was one of the major weaknesses of qualitative research, and, moreover, is one of the reasons why I felt it would be valuable to include a quantitative analysis of the previously launched adult phenomenon for this book.

Chapter 6
Conclusion

Abstract This chapter concludes the book by providing a restatement of the phenomenon of previously launched adults, the quantitative and qualitative results, relevance of the topic under study, and suggestions for future areas of research regarding families and adult child–parent coresidence.

Keywords Conclusion • Families • Child • Parent

My quantitative research had three main objectives: the first was to examine the relationship between different life course variables and launching status; the second was to examine the relationship between family development and family structure variables and launching status; and the last objective was to use descriptive statistics to simply describe more current trends of young adult and parent coresidence. In this chapter I will discuss the hypotheses of the models tested in this research and summarize my main research and findings. I will first discuss some of the principal results from Chap. 4, which reported the results of the multinomial logistic regression models using launching status as the dependent variable.

6.1 Summary of Results

6.1.1 Life Course Development Framework

Chapter 4 first used the dependent variable launching status to examine the relationship between various life course variables and the launching status of a young adult. The analyses of this chapter tested various hypotheses related to different life course variables and found that many of the life course variables were significantly associated with launching status, even with the addition of control variables. Child's age, child's marital status, child's number of children, child's sex and child's income were all significantly associated with the risk of being a failure to launch adult. Additionally, I found that child's age, child's marital status, and sex were significantly associated with a child being a previously launched adult. As expected, most of the life course variables were significantly related to launching status. Many of

© Springer International Publishing Switzerland 2016

D.N. Farris, *Boomerang Kids: The Demography of Previously Launched Adults*, SpringerBriefs in Population Studies, DOI 10.1007/978-3-319-31227-9_6 my hypotheses proved correct in the analysis of the life course variables. In the model for failure to launch, the variable of child's marital status has a relative risk ratio of 11.1 indicating a very strong positive effect of marital status. In the model for previously launched adults, the marital status variable is also positive but not as strong as in the previous model. In the failure to launch model, the variable for child's number of children has a relative risk ratio of .67. The greater the number of children, the less the risk.

Despite many significant and correct hypotheses, my hypothesis regarding parent's age was not supported. My hypothesis regarding child's age was supported and age was proven to be significantly associated with launching status in the failure to launch model. However, in the previously launched model, contrary to my hypothesis, older adults were more likely to move back in with their parents and this finding was significant. Thus, my hypothesis was confirmed for only one group of adult children.

I hypothesized that both adult children who were married and those with children would be less likely to live at home. My hypothesis for marital status was supported and significant in both models; however my hypothesis for number of children was only significant in the model for failure to launch.

My hypothesis for education was also supported; however the results were not significant. My hypothesis regarding sex was interesting in that males were shown to be more likely to be living at home than females, but this was only the case for those who were failures to launch. My hypothesis that adult children with higher incomes would be less likely to move back home was supported for failure to launch adults, but not supported for previously launched adults. However, with the failure to launch model this variable was significant and in the previously launched model it was not significant. I will now turn to a discussion of the family development framework analysis for the data from Wave 3.

6.1.2 Family Development Framework

As discussed in Chap. 4, several variables related to family development were not shown to have any significant association with launching status. In the model for failure to launch, parent's marital status, number of siblings, parent's health, how well the child gets along with the mother, and how well the child gets along with the father were all shown to not have any significant association with launching status. However, in the model for previously launching status, only parent's marital status, the second variable relating to parent's health and well being, and how well the adult child gets along with their mother and income were not significantly associated with launching status.

For the failure to launch category, the only variables that were significantly associated with launching status were sex, income, and age, all of which were used as control variables in the models. For the previously launched category, number of siblings, parent's health, how well the adult child gets along with their father, sex, and age were significantly associated with launching status.

As I stated, support for my hypotheses in the family development model had varying degrees of success. This finding regarding number of siblings was inconsistent with my hypothesis that adult children would be less likely to live at home if they had more siblings. Regarding parent's health, I found that healthier the parent, the less the risk of being a previously launched adult. This finding is consistent with my hypothesis. Contrary to my hypothesis, in which I had predicted that adult children would be more likely to live at home if they got along well with their parents, I found that this variable worked in the opposite direction.

Some of my hypotheses relating to the family development framework andfamily structure were supported, but others were not. However many of the variables did not turn out to be significant with the addition of the control variables. Prior to the addition of control variables in the models, parent's health and well-being was shown to be significantly associated with launching status, namely the launching status of failure to launch; however as the parent was more dissatisfied with themselves they are less likely to have an adult child living at home, which was contrary to my hypothesis. For previously launched adults, the hypothesis relating to number of siblings was significantly associated with previously launched adults launching status, which also was inconsistent with my expectations. Additionally, parent's health and well being (1) was proven to be significantly related to launching status and in the direction predicted. How well the adult child got along with the father was also significant, albeit in a direction opposite to that expected. I had hypothesized that variables relating to the family would significantly impact the launching status of young adults; clearly, my hypotheses were not supported with the data.

Overall, I believe that the findings of the multinomial logistic regression analyses in Chap. 4 show support for the idea that there is a legitimate connection between life course variables and launching status of adult children. Contrarily, I also think that the findings of the analyses show support for the idea that the family development and family structure variables do not have a very legitimate connection to launching status of adult children.

I feel that the support of the life course framework theory in this research is very important. We can see that per the results of my analysis, there are some very strong and significant relationships between various events or statuses in the life course and the launching status of the adult child. In terms of different stages of the life course and their relationship to launching status, we see that the variables had, in some cases, different effects depending on which launching status was being analyzed. I feel like the strong support for the hypotheses related to the life course perspective are important for a variety of reasons. I feel that these results lend credence to the notion that there is a powerful connection between individual lives and the historical and socioeconomic contexts in which these lives unfold (Mitchell

2006). It is important to note that different variations in social contexts, including family structure, background, and different demographic variables (such as race, gender, religion, occupation, and social class) can have profound ramifications on an individual's particular pattern in the life course and I feel that these different variables were shown to be significant in this analysis.

Elder has argued that various historical forces "shape the social trajectories of family, education, and work, and they in turn influence behavior and particular lines of development" (1998: 2). Likewise, Mitchell (2006) has argued that an individual's own life path is embedded in and transformed by conditions and events occurring during the historical period and geographical location in which the person lives. Geopolitical events, economic cycles, and social and cultural ideologies can often shape people's perceptions and choices and alter the course of human development. I believe that the historical forces at work that need to be entertained in my research are the economic crises that have shaped the last ten or so years, most especially in the years between 2005 and 2010. Various contributing factors include the bursting of the housing bubble, sub-prime and predatory lending, and increased debt; indeed all may be active parts of history that would be historical factors that changed history in a negative way. We can see that all of these various interrelated parts are combined in a way that led to economic downturn; this in turn has led to decreased job opportunities for young adults, high student loan debt, and lack of viable prospects for the future. Next I will turn to a summary and discussion of the descriptive results I obtained by analyzing the 2009 American Community Survey.

6.1.3   Descriptive Results, 2009 American Community Survey

In Chap. 4 I employed the use of a supplemental analysis of ACS data because I felt it was important to be able to look at more recent trends of adult child and parent coresidence. I analyzed at various demographic characteristics of young adults that lived at home. A majority of the young adults were between the ages of 18 and 24. Additionally, a majority of the young adults were white, non-Hispanic, male, and had a high school diploma or less educational attainment.

Because of the recent release of the data, I was able describe some of the more up to date trends of young adults living with their parents. Unfortunately, the ACS data do not differentiate between adult children who have never moved out of the family home and those who have moved out and then returned; rather, they just describe the current living situation of the head of the household and others in the household. For the purposes of merely describing the trends of young adults living with their parents, this lack of distinction between the two groups appears to be satisfactory.

6.2 Discussion and Future Research

Future research could address the long-term implications of moving back in with parents. A longitudinal study would be an interesting way to follow respondents to see how this break in the life course effects other transitions in the life. Examining the differences in those who move back home as related to temporal length of stay, number of returns, and feelings about the situation as related to the individual's age could provide more insight about previously launched adults.

6.3 Conclusion

Adult children living with their parents is and will continue to be an important area of research in sociological and demographic studies, particularly in light of a poor economic situation, rising costs of living, poor job opportunities and high debt. Not only is adult child and parent coresidence an especially relevant issue, it can have an effect on a variety of demographic outcomes as well. The largest implication of this research relates to the life course variables and how these influence the launching status of adult children. Obviously, the changes in the life course are directly related to the economic situation of our times. Life course trajectory assumed that young adults were expected to transition to adulthood on a linear path of well-timed events, such as employment, marriage, and parenting (Elder 1998). However, several aspects of this trajectory are variable among the youth population of today. Children are graduating from high school or college, getting jobs or continuing schooling, but moving back home and delaying marriage and families. Parents are becoming more accommodating of this, and children returning home may not be as big of an issue as it once was.

One of the major strengths of this study is the relevancy of the issue to the current events in our nation. The phenomenon of adult children moving back home is becoming more prevalent than ever, and the existence and continually growing number of this group is merit enough for research. There is certainly potential for the emergence of more adult children moving back home. The nature of this research allowed me to investigate various contributing factors and independent variables that lead adult children to either never move out of the family home or to move out and subsequently return.

In the qualitative research I conducted, I investigated the experiences and emotions of individuals who had moved back in with their parents and the parents themselves, and the quantitative aspect of this book is the perfect complement to this qualitative work. By looking at the association of launching status and various life course and family development variables, I was able to see what people were more likely to be failure to launch or previously launched adults. I find this particular area of study to be not only relevant but also quite interesting, and it is my feeling that sociologists, economists, and non-academics would find further analysis of this topic to be both enlightening and important.

References

Aldous, J. (1978). *Family careers: Developmental change in families*. New York: John Wiley & Sons.

Aquilino, W. S. (1990). The likelihood of parent- adult child coresidence: Effects of family structure and parental characteristics. *Journal of Marriage and Family, 52*, 405–419.

Aquilino, W. S. (1991). Predicting parents' experiences with coresident adult children. *Journal of Family Issues, 12*, 323–342.

Aquilino, W. S., & Supple, K. R. (1991). Parent–child relations and parents' satisfaction when adult children live at home. *Journal of Marriage and the Family, 53*, 13–27.

Arnett, J. (2000). Emerging adulthood: A theory of development from the late teens through the twenties. *American Psychologist, 55*, 469–480.

Baumeister, R. F., Campbell, J. D., Krueger, J. I., & Vohs, K. D. (2003). Does high self esteem cause better performance, interpersonal success, happiness, or healthier lifestyles? *Psychological Science in the Public Interest, 4*, 1–44.

Billari, F. C., & Liefbroer, A. C. (2007). Should I stay or should I go? The impact of age norms on leaving home. *Demography, 44*, 181–198.

Blau, P. M. (1964). *Exchange and power in social life*. New York: Wiley.

Bordieu, P. (1986). The forms of capital. In J. Richardson (Ed.), *Handbook of theory and research for the sociology of education* (pp. 241–258). New York: Greenwood.

Buunk, A. P., Groothof, H. A., & Siero, F. W. (2007). Social comparison and satisfaction with one's social life. *Journal of Social and Personal Relationships, 24*, 197–205.

Cast, A. D., & Burke, P. J. (2002). A theory of self esteem. *Social Forces, 80*, 1041–1068.

Cherlin, A. J. (2009). *The marriage go round: The state of marriage and family in America today*. New York: Alfred A. Knopf.

Clausen, J. A. (1972). The life course of individuals. In M. W. Riley, M. E. Johnson, & A. Foner (Eds.), *Aging and society: A sociology of age stratification* (pp. 457–514). New York: Russell Sage Foundation.

Clemens, A. W., & Axelson, L. J. (1985). The not so empty nest: The return of the fledgling adult. *Family Relations, 34*, 259–264.

Coltrane, S. (2000). Research on household labor: Modeling and measuring the social embeddedness of routine family work. *Journal of Marriage and Family, 62*, 4.

Cooley, C. H. (1902). *Human nature and the social order*. New York: Scribner's.

Crocker, J., Brook, A. T., Yu, N., & Villacorta, M. (2006). The pursuit of self esteem: Contingencies of self worth and self regulation. *Journal of Personality, 74*, 1749–1772.

Davis, K. (1963). The theory of change and response in modern demographic history. *Population Index, 29*, 345–366.

© Springer International Publishing Switzerland 2016

D.N. Farris, *Boomerang Kids: The Demography of Previously Launched Adults*, SpringerBriefs in Population Studies, DOI 10.1007/978-3-319-31227-9

Elder, G. (1985). *Life course dynamics: Trajectories and transitions, 1968–1980*. Ithaca: Cornell University Press.

Elder, G. (1998). The life course as developmental theory. *Child Development, 69*, 1–12.

Esterberg, K. (2001). *Qualitative methods in social research*. Boston: McGraw Hill.

Fishbein, M., & Ajzen, I. (1975). *Belief, attitude, intention and behavior: An introduction to theory and research*. Reading: Addison-Wesley.

Franks, D., & Marolla, J. (1976). Efficacious action and social approval as interacting dimensions of self esteem: A tentative formulation through construct validation. *Sociometry, 39*, 324–341.

Furman, E. (2005). *Boomerang nation: How to survive living with your parents... The second time around*. New York: Fireside.

Goffman, E. (1963). *Stigma: Notes on the management of spoiled identity*. Englewood Cliffs: Prentice Hall.

Goldscheider, F. K., & DeVanzo, J. (1985). Living arrangements and the transition to adulthood. *Demography, 22*, 545–563.

Goldscheider, F. K., & Goldscheider, C. (1989). Family structure and conflict: Nest- leaving expectations of young adults and their parents. *Journal of Marriage and the Family, 51*, 1.

Goldscheider, F. K., & Goldscheider, C. (1998). The effects of childhood family structure on leaving and returning home. *Journal of Marriage and the Family, 60*, 745–756.

Goldscheider, F. K., & Goldscheider, C. (1999). *The changing transition to adulthood: Leaving and returning home: Understanding families* (Vol. 17). Thousand Oaks: Sage Publications.

Hamilton, L. C. (1992). *Regression with graphics: A second course in applied statistics*. Belmont: Duxbury Press.

Henig, R. M. (2010). The post-adolescent, pre-adult, not-quite-decided life stage. *The New York Times Magazine, 22*, 30–37.

Hess, B. B. (1988). Social structures and human lives: A sociological theme. In M. W. Riley (Ed.), *Social structures & human lives*. Newberry Park: SAGE Publications, Inc.

Hochschild, A., & Machung, A. (1989). *The second shift: Working families and the revolution at home*. New York: Viking Penguin.

Hogg, M. A., & Reid, S. A. (2006). Social identity, self categorization, and the communication of group norms. *Communication Theory, 16*, 7–30.

Hondagneu-Sotelo, P. (2007). *Domestica: Immigrant workers cleaning and caring in the shadows of affluence*. Berkeley and Los Angeles: University of California Press, Ltd.

Howard, J. A. (2000). Social psychology of identities. *Annual Review of Sociology, 26*, 367–393.

Landale, N. S., & Oropesa, R. S. (2007). Hispanic families: Stability and change. *Annual Review of Sociology, 33*, 381–405.

Long, S. J., & Freese, J. (2003). *Regression models for categorical dependent variables using Stata*. College Station: Stata Press.

Lundgren, D. C. (2004). Social feedback and self appraisals: Current status of the Mead-Cooley Hypothesis. *Symbolic Interaction, 27*, 267–286.

Matza, D., & Sykes, G. M. (1957). Techniques of neutralization: A theory of delinquency. *American Sociological Review, 22*, 664–670.

Mead, G. H. (1934). *Mind, self, and society*. Chicago: University of Chicago Press.

Menard, S. (2002). *Applied logistic regression analysis*. Thousand Oaks: Sage.

Milkie, M., Bianchi, S. M., Mattingly, M., & Robinson, J. P. (2002). Gendered division of childrearing: Ideals, realities, and the relationship to parental well being. *Sex Roles, 47*, 1–2.

Mitchell, B. (1998). Too close for comfort? Parental assessments of 'Boomerang Kid' living arrangements. *Canadian Journal of Sociology, 23*, 21–47.

Mitchell, B. (2000). The refilled nest: Debunking the myth of families in crisis. In E. M. Gee & G. Gutman (Eds.), *The overselling of population aging: Apocalyptic demography and intergenerational challenges* (pp. 80–99). Toronto: Oxford University Press.

Mitchell, B. (2006). *The boomerang age: Transitions to adulthood in families*. Piscataway: Aldine Transaction.

Mitchell, B. (2009). *Family matters: An introduction to family sociology in Canada*. Toronto: Canadian Scholars Press.

Mitchell, B., & Gee, E. M. (1996). 'Boomerang Kids' and midlife parental marital satisfaction. *Family Relations, 45*, 442–448.

Poston, D. L., Jr., & Bouvier, L. (2010). *Population and society: An introduction to demography*. New York: Cambridge University Press.

Rindfuss, R. (1991). *The young adult years: Diversity, structural change, and fertility*. Population Association of America Presidential Address. Reprinted in *Demography* 28:4.

Rosenfeld, M. J. (2007). *The age of independence: Interracial unions, same-sex unions and the changing American family*. Cambridge, MA: Harvard University Press.

Rubin, M., & Hewstone, M. (1998). Social identity theory's self-esteem hypothesis: A review and some suggestions for clarification. *Personality and Social Psychology Review, 2*, 40–63.

Schnaiberg, A., & Goldenberg, S. (1989). From empty nest to crowded nest: The dynamics of incompletely launched young adults. *Social Problems, 36*, 251–269.

Settersten, R. A. (1998). Time, age, and the transition to retirement: New evidence on life course flexibility? *The International Journal of Aging and Human Development, 47*, 177–203.

Settersten, R. A., Jr., & Hagestad, G. O. (1996). What's the latest? Cultural age deadlines for family transitions. *The Gerontologist, 36*, 602–613.

Smith, T. W. (2004). Coming of Age in twenty first century America: Public attitudes towards the importance and timing of transitions to adulthood. *Ageing International, 29*, 136–148.

Speare, A., Jr., & Avery, R. (1992). *Changes in parent–child coresidence in later life*. Paper presented at the annual scientific meeting of the Gerontological Society of America in San Francisco, November 22–26, 1991.

Sweet, J., & Bumpass, L. (1995). *Cohabitation, marriage and union stability: Preliminary findings from NSFH2* (NSFH Working Paper No. 65). Madison: University of Wisconsin-Madison.

Sweet, J., Bumpass, L., & Call, V. (1988). *The design and content of the National Survey of Families and Households* (NSFH working paper No. 1). Madison: University of Wisconsin-Madison.

Treiman, D. J. (2009). *Quantitative data analysis: Doing social research to test ideas*. San Francisco: Jossey-Bass.

United States Bureau of the Census. (2010a). *American community survey design methodology*. Retrieved July 1, 2010, http://www.census.gov/acs/www/methodology/methodology_main/

United States Bureau of the Census. (2010b). *Table MS-2. Estimated median age at first marriage*. Retrieved July 1, 2010, www.census.gov/population/socdemo/hh-fam/ms2.pdf

United States Bureau of the Census. (2014). *New census bureau statistics show how young adults today compare with previous generations in neighborhoods nationwide*. Retrieved June 8, 2015, http://www.census.gov/newsroom/press-releases/2014/cb14-219.html

Veevers, J. E., Gee, E. M., & Wister, A. V. (1996). Homeleaving Age norms: Conflict or consensus? *International Journal of Aging and Human Development, 43*, 1–19.

Waite, L. J. (2006). Marriage and family. In M. Micklin & D. L. Poston Jr. (Eds.), *Handbook of population* (pp. 87–108). New York: Springer.

White, L. (1994). Coresidence and living at home: Young adults and their parents. *Annual Review of Sociology, 20*, 81–102.

Wolf, J. B. (2007). Is breast really best? Risk and total motherhood in the national breastfeeding awareness campaign. *Journal of Health Politics, Policy and Law, 32*, 4.

67138707R00051

Made in the USA
Lexington, KY
02 September 2017